Katrin Beh... S0-BNR-908

Indoor Cats

Understanding and Caring for Your Indoor Cat

With 30 color photographs by
Ulrike Schanz

Drawings by Renate Holzner

Translated from the German by
Elizabeth D. Crawford

Consulting Editor: J. Anne Helgren

BARRON'S

Contents

Title page: A window shelf over a heating unit is the established favorite spot of these two cats. It's beautifully warm here, with a good view of everying.

The cat loves to play with a hard rubber ball, empty spools, or fur mice.

Preface

Cats love being cozy more than anything and can thus be very happy living exclusively indoors. However, to remain physically fit and to avoid psychological damage from confinement, they need their owners to provide additional play, occupation, and exercise.

In this book, cat expert Katrin Behrend explains how to provide proper care and maintenance for indoor cats. She gives tips on how to find the cat best suited to you and how to arrange your home in the best way for your cat. Artist Renate Holzner presents a graphic view of how an adventure-filled playground for kitty might look. In addition, you'll learn about acclimating your cat, feeding your cat a proper diet, and what is important for maintaining its health. In the chapter "Learning to Understand Cats," feline behavior patterns are explained so that you can establish a positive relationship with your cat from the beginning. The How-To sections give you information about a health checkup for your cat, the important grooming procedures, tried-and-true training practices, playing with your cat, cat menus, and the language of cats, all enhanced by graphic illustrations. In addition, the color photographs taken especially for this book provide a living picture of these fascinating animals. The author and the publisher wish you great pleasure with your indoor cat.

Interesting Information About Indoor Cats

Goddess and Witch

In the New Kingdom of Egypt around 1500 B.C. the dun-colored African wildcat, *Felis libyca,* first approached human beings, lured by the quantities of rats and mice that threatened the gigantic wheat and rice stores of the Egyptians. The cat attached itself to humans, turning itself into a pet. And the humans recognized the uniqueness of the event and made the cat into a goddess.

Besides admiring the cat's universally prized ability to contain the rodents feared as destroyers of food supplies and carriers of disease, human beings saw her as a reserved, unfathomable species; something worthy of worship. She was honored as the mild, kind goddess Bastet, wife of the sun god Ra, and was represented with the body of a woman and the head of a cat. She had her own temples and cemeteries, and anyone who killed or injured a cat was punished with death. When people in other countries also learned of her value as a mouser, her triumphal march throughout the rest of the world began. The cat was considered something special everywhere; people marveled at the incomparable mixture of independent predator and gentle, affectionate creature.

But then her troubles began. Dark times arose for the cat in Europe during the Middle Ages. Her problem was that she remained mysterious and unfathomable and became connected with heathen practices. Along with some women, millions of cats became the victims of witch hunts, and the conse-

The cat, that extraordinary creature! You may admire its independence and enjoy its affection.

quences for humans were fatal. For then there was nothing to control the rats, which introduced the plague into medieval cities. Now the persecutors of cats were destroyed, also by the millions. It took until well into the eighteenth century before the cat's resurgence as a popular house pet began; it is still going on today.

Beloved Pet

The role played by painters and poets in the rehabilitation of the cat is not an insignificant one. The cat was promoted to the animal of the artist. It became a lead actor in countless stories, because particularly among writers one finds unreserved cat lovers who admire the cat's independence and self-assurance. Authors made cats into main characters in their novels and paid tribute to them and their social value. This began with the story of "Puss in Boots" by the Frenchman Charles Perrault. The story appeared in 1698 and showed the cat in an entirely new light. The hated witches' animal had become a friend of humans.

What the country folk, who prized the services of the cat as a mouser, had long known now penetrated the consciousness of the educated and the nobility. They turned their attention toward the cat and kept especially beautiful specimens in the house as status symbols. For instance, Angora cats, which were introduced from Turkey to France and England, were much sought after because people so admired their silky coats. With the introduction of hygiene

All ears and eyes and body are tensed—something's going on that's extremely interesting to kitty.

into the household, people prized the cat even more for its fastidious habits. After the first cat show in London in 1871 and after the foundation of cat clubs in England and America at the end of the nineteenth century and the beginning of systematic breeding, the popularity of the cat as a pet increased more and more. Numbers indicate that in recent years cats have even overtaken dogs in the favor of animal lovers. So the former goddess Bastet has turned into the popular house-tiger to whom, without a complaint, one concedes the most comfortable chair in the living room.

A n indoor cat leads a longer, better-protected life than a cat that is exposed to the dangers of the streets, the farmyard, or the forests and country side.

Indoor Cats—Cats Without Freedom

The cat has its own way of reacting to circumstances. As much as it's a loner, it still doesn't want to do without the society of humans. When, with progressive urbanization, people are living more and more in apartments, the cat goes along with them.

With tail held high, head raised, and joyous meow, the cat greets "its" people.

Unfortunately, city life is full of dangers for cats, and so people feel compelled to keep them in the apartment for protection. "You're imprisoning them," say the opponents of this practice, but the cat obviously doesn't see it that way. Expressed the other way around, the cat succeeds in adapting without changing its nature.

All the same, now and then you may ask how the cat's life would be in the wild. This is how: A cat spends a large portion of the day sleeping or resting. When it's awake, it sharpens its claws, seeks out hiding places, reconnoiters its territory, satisfies its hunger, and carries on a social life, if it happens to be in the mood at the time. If you permit the cat to engage in these activities within four walls, kitty "snuggles down" without any trouble.

Given room to stretch its legs, several niches into which to withdraw, an observation spot at a window or on a balcony, toys for occupation, in addition to your loving care and attention, and your cat will enjoy a diverse, happy, and comfortable existence with you. Furthermore, an indoor cat can live a longer and safer life than a "free" cat—a powerful advantage compared with the outdoor cat that can no longer stroll around alone without encountering danger, even in country regions.

Do They Miss Their Freedom?

There's great controversy about whether indoor-only cats miss their freedom. I think not. If they were kept indoors from the time they were small, they don't have the urge for it. Indeed, they're completely overwhelmed when you provide them with an excursion to the country every now and then. It's somewhat different when they regularly have a chance to enjoy running

Which Cat Is Right for You?

Whether the animal is black, red, or a striped house cat or an exotic purebred, the question is temperament. The following descriptions and advice should help you to find the cat that suits you. But if your cat turns out to be somewhat different anyway, don't hold it against your pet. It's just not possible to give exact recipes for such a many-sided creature.

Cat Temperaments	Tips for Getting Acquainted	Breeds with These Characteristics
The sociable cat, after a short period of holding back, will approach you amiably, let you stroke it, and let you scratch its head. It is curious, active, and playful, and bonds easily with children.	Don't push. Wait until the cat voluntarily comes to you for cuddling or playing.	Maine coon, Norwegian forest cat, Turkish Angora, Somali, Burmese, Ragdoll, Scottish Fold
The quiet cat is even tempered and agreeable in the circle of its kitten siblings. It takes time to initiate contact because the cat sniffs all around calmly and will not be hurried.	This cat stands its ground, that is to say, it doesn't withdraw to observe. If you recognize this little difference, you know with whom you are dealing.	Persian, Chartreux (British shorthair), Exotic shorthair
The shy cat at first withdraws into a safe corner and observes from there. When the ice is broken, it bonds particularly closely to "its" people.	You shouldn't rush into anything with this cat. Demonstrate with treats that it is your special friend. But you also mustn't let this cat down, since it can be very difficult to reestablish trust.	
The capricious cat loves to be at the center and can sulk for hours at lack of attention. This ultra-temperamental cat type is very attached to humans and needs much attention.	Such characteristics are rather typical for particular breeds. You should take this into consideration before you make your choice.	Abyssinian, Burmese, Oriental shorthair, Rex, Russian blue, Siamese

A cat radiates calm when it is cuddled up to its person and purring.

free every weekend or on vacation. They can readily adapt to situations that then become routine. Thus, my cats romp around at will in the piazza during vacations at our house in Italy, but they know how to pass the time that they spend the rest of the year in my apartment. Even when they spent a whole year living in Italy, they weren't "strangers" to the old apartment because the moment we returned they, without hesitation, resumed their usual places.

Before You Get a Cat

Will a Cat Fit Into Your Life?

A cat really will adapt to any household, whether it consists of one or several people, young or old. However, there are a few things you should consider before getting your new apartment mate. After all, you'll have to deal with a headstrong personality for the next 12 to 15 years, sometimes even longer.

Single: People who live alone and are independent plan their lives differently from those with family ties. Therefore, you should consider beforehand whether keeping a cat will fit in with your own future plans. What happens if a partner appears who doesn't like your cat? If you have to travel for business or vacation (see page 32)? If you have to go to the hospital or nursing home?

Older people: For older people, cats, by their nature, are often extraordinarily calming because they radiate infinite calm. They are a comfort in loneliness, aren't demanding and excitable, and can be cared for without difficulty. Still, in this case you should also consider beforehand what is to be done if you want to travel. Also consider what will happen if you have to go into the hospital, a nursing home, or retirement home, which unfortunately you can't plan ahead of time.

My tip: If you take an older cat, for instance from an animal shelter you shorten the length of time in which you'll be responsible for it.

Family: A cat can adjust to even the most turbulent household, provided that you haven't chosen an overanxious type. Children learn in dealing with cats

to respect the personality of the animal. It should be decided ahead of time who is going to take care of the cat, and regularly put out its food and clean its litter box.

My tip: If you have very small children but you want them to be able to grow up with an animal, get a young adolescent cat. It should be accustomed to human contact and be loving and gentle. Such a cat is more likely to endure the clumsy grasp of small children's hands without scratching and biting (see Cats and Children, page 25).

Five Questions for the Cat Lover

1. Are you ready to give your cat enough variety and occupation indoors that its innate behavior patterns are not excessively constricted? Even if the animal doesn't mind the decreased exercise area, it has certain territorial requirements (see A Home to a Cat's Taste, page 15).

2. Will it disturb you if the cat sheds on the carpet or couch after grooming itself? If it vomits up the hairs it swallowed during grooming and often seeks out the carpet to do it? When it tracks cat litter throughout the home and leaves "messes" around its dish? These are all normal feline characteristics and behavior patterns.

3. Do you understand that a cat must be regularly immunized (see page 46), and that this costs money in addition to the cost of feeding and maintenance?

4. If you live in an apartment, have you checked with your landlord? Many

Before you get a cat, you should understand that for the next 15 to 20 years you will be dealing with a headstrong personality and bear the responsibility for it.

leases contain restrictions regarding pets, so you should make sure to find out beforehand.

5. Are you or another family member allergic to cat hair? People with an allergy to animal fur should not keep cats.

How You Get a Cat

Kittens: You may find kittens through friends, neighbors, animal shelters or from posted notices in pet supply stores. In any case, you should play with the kittens extensively and finally choose the one that seems to suit you and your family best. But there are many things that affect the character of the kitten. For instance, if a mother cat trusts "her" people, she transmits that trust to her children.

My tip: Follow the development of the young to get a picture of an individual type. See what they do in the scuffle for their mother's nipple, how the kittens play with each other, how well they manage using the litter box, and whether they are shy with visitors.

Purebred cats: You not only must pay a lot of money for a purebred cat, but

you must also have fallen in love with a particular type, which is primarily recognized by appearance. Find out ahead of time whether this breed suits you. It's best to buy from a breeder (see Useful Addresses, page 61) or from a good pet dealer. Make sure you get a pedigree and an immunization certificate with it and find out if the kitten has been wormed (see HOW-TO: The Health Checkup, page 26).

Animal shelter cats: Stray or abandoned animals are supplied by animal shelters, humane societies, or private cat rescue organizations. The price of adoption usually only covers the expenses, because practically all cats are immunized, wormed, and spayed or neutered on admission. However, only cats that have already lived with people are suitable for keeping indoors.

My tip: Try to find out as much as possible about the animal's past. Observe whether the cat spits or retreats or, rather, comes to you when you approach it.

Cats from newspaper advertisements: Unfortunately there are many different motivations behind the notices appearing under the heading "Pet Sales." There are the cat lovers who really are concerned about good homes for their kittens. Many give away kittens without charge, or it may be that they have already had them immunized as well as wormed and want these outlays reimbursed. Then there are the profiteers, who let their cats have kittens as often

Head rubbing is a form of approach. The cat rubs its cheeks or forehead on a person's hand.

as possible only to make money. They ask for a fee—which simply means the selling price—and usually haven't had the kittens immunized. Also, often there are advertisements by purebred cat owners who have so-called fanciers' cats available, as well as breeders who pursue the business professionally (see Purebred cats, above).

Cats from the pet store: Usually what's involved in pet store purchases are spontaneous sales, because you've fallen in love with one of the frisky, clumsy, romping kittens. These are usually purebred cats, but it isn't only because of the price that caution is suggested. Look around the store carefully, for, unfortunately, there are sharp operators in this area as well. Good pet dealers will keep their cats clean and supplied with toys and things to cuddle with and, besides providing them with a proper diet, will also give them the necessary attention. Furthermore, they will give you good advice on making a choice.

Stray cats: Usually you find a masterless stray on the streets of your town or perhaps even on your doorstep, injured beside the road, or on a trip to the countryside. Beyond the first rush of pity, you should bear in mind that you know nothing about the animal's past and it may possibly never get used to life indoors. On the other hand, you may become best friends.

Male or Female?

I haven't been able to observe gender-specific behavior characteristics in my cats. The tomcat was a real sweetheart, but the two females are also extraordinarily affectionate when they want to be petted. You should think about the following:

A female becomes sexually mature between six and 12 months of age and

This is the proper way to lift a cat. To carry, take the cat in the crook of your arm and hold it firmly with your other hand.

then is in heat two to three times a year, that is to say, she's ready to breed. Because indoors she usually doesn't meet up with any males, she remains in the mood for love for ten days, sometimes even for two or three weeks. When heat begins, the queen will meow and howl insistently; this distinctive sound is called "calling." She will roll on the ground and rub up against you and items in your home. The queen may assume the mating position called lordosis; she crouches down with her back swayed and her tail held to one side, and treads with her rear feet. She may also pace back and forth and seem restless and agitated.

A male becomes sexually mature at about the age of nine months and then begins to mark his territory by spraying urine everywhere. The odor is nearly

A scratching or playing tree like this offers the cat constant variety.

places, a food dish that's always full, and a territory that no one contests—where from a cat's point of view are the challenges? Many cats, alone all day long because "their" humans have to go to work, become quite bored. If a friendship develops between them, two cats kept together exercise, wrestle, play, and cuddle each other. Not to worry, that doesn't mean they'll ignore you—they'll harmoniously "possess" you whenever they feel like it.

Some possibilities are:
• two siblings from one litter;
• an older and a young cat, but the new one should have a temperament that harmonizes with that of the old inhabitant;
• two adult cats; for these you need a great deal of intuition in order to get them used to one another and enough room so they can each establish their own territories.

Cats and Other Cats

Getting an old, established cat to be friends with a new kitten is a matter that must be managed by instinct. The old cat regards the home in which it has ruled alone until now as its kingdom and he will defend the territory with tooth and claw. Outdoors, the new arrival would respect this and unobtrusively disappear into the bushes. Indoors, that doesn't work, and so the old cat responds by becoming defensive, acting offended, possibly even by developing behavior problems such as loss of appetite or doing its business in the middle of the rug. (See Old Cats and New Arrivals, page 24)

Note: Sometimes the old, established cat doesn't terrorize the new one but the other way around. If you can't overcome this problem, I recommend that you find a new home for the new cat as quickly as possible.

impossible to remove from furniture and carpets. You avoid these problems if you have the animals neutered (see page 28). Have your male cat neutered young—at approximately six to nine months of age. If you wait until spraying becomes a habit, neutering may not stop this behavior.

One or Two?

A cat that lives indoors always has a safe roof over its head (unless you live in the earthquake belt of the West Coast), comfortable, warm resting

Cats and Other Household Pets

Cats have no fear of animals that are smaller than they are, but they may see them as prey or playthings.

On the other hand, they count animals that are as large or larger as enemies, at least until the cat can win them over.

Dogs: If you already have a dog, there will be hardly any special difficulties (unless the dog has already had a bad experience with an enemy cat).

The supposed genetic enmity between dog and cat is really a fairy tale. Animosity between the two animals is actually triggered through "language difficulties." In the dog, tail wagging means readiness for contact, a friendly mood, whereas with cats, tail lashing signals tense alertness but also irritation and aggressiveness.

Dogs sniff each other's anus the first time they meet. Cats are by nature more reserved, and only after some time do they sniff nose to nose. Cats perceive the dog's rapid approach as an attack, and they react by hissing, spitting, or threatening to scratch, or by lifting a threatening paw. On the other hand, to the dog this means, play with me.

It works well when two animals are raised together from infancy or when a young kitten is introduced to an adult dog. It works only on occasion or not at all when a young dog is introduced to an adult cat that is used to being the center of attention. The cat can so intimidate the dog that it turns into an anxious, unhappy animal that is always creeping about.

Guinea pigs and hamsters: Cats can make friends with guinea pigs, but you shouldn't count on it. They will probably view hamsters as prey.

Dwarf rabbits: Both dwarf rabbits and cats can eventually get used to each other.

Chasing a toy mouse is a typical cat game.

Smaller parakeets, budgies, and canaries: Cats hunt birds and eat them. Sometimes, however, there can also be friendships formed.

Parrots and larger parakeets: These psittacines can become jealous and injure the cat with their beak; on the other hand, the cat can swat at them and bite them.

All the Things a Cat Needs

A few items should already be on hand and in their rightful places by the time your new companion comes into your home. The cat can then sniff them on the first exploratory round and get used to them.

Cat bed: No cat can resist a cat bed. Your pet will immediately climb in and make itself comfortable. The bed needn't be luxuriously upholstered, a piece of soft material is enough. However, that's not to say that the cat will spend the entire night there. A cat will always seek out several comfortable resting places for itself.

Litter box: There are three forms of litter box available in pet stores:
• the simple plastic pan, which is also good for traveling;
• the plastic pan with a rim attached so that the litter isn't so easily scattered outside the pan;
• the litter box "house" with a fitted plastic dome cover to give the cat privacy, contain the litter, and help control odor.

In addition to this are:
• cat litter: It is usually odor-controlling. Available in bags of 5 to 20 pounds (2.3–9 kg). The clumping clay litter available in pet stores is environmentally safe and can be disposed of with the garbage. It is economical to use, because the excrement forms clumps, which can be removed.
• a plastic or metal scoop with which you remove the wastes and soiled litter from the pan and throw them in the garbage.

My tip: There are suppliers who will supply cat litter and food directly to your home. You can find the addresses in a pet supply store or cat magazine.

Cat trees and scratching posts: So the cat doesn't sharpen its claws on the rug, carpet, or upholstered furniture, you need a cat tree or scratching post (see Arranging Your Home for a Cat, page 16).
• Cat trees can be simple posts or elaborate "condos." On the fancy models, the trunk is covered with sisal rope or carpeting, and perches and enclosed cuddly "caves" at various heights invite climbing, sitting, and sleeping (the pet supply store offers the most varieties). The scratching tree or post must be stable and is best fastened to the floor and wall or ceiling with angle irons.
• Scratching boards: These are flat pieces of wood or heavy cardboard that can be fastened to walls, furniture, or doorknobs at a height the cat can reach. A thick, slide-proof doormat of sisal will do as well, or a piece of scrap carpeting with the jute backing side up.

Food and water dishes: You need one to two feeding dishes for each cat (for fresh and dry food) and a water dish. How they look and what they are made of doesn't matter to the cat, they must only be as stable as possible and nonsliding.

Cat grass: Cats need "greenstuff," probably to help them vomit up the hair they've swallowed during grooming. It's a good idea to provide them with grass grown specially for them (you can get grass kits from the pet supply store) because many plants in your home are poisonous to cats (see How to Make the Home Safe for Cats, page 22).

There's good climbing and claw sharpening on a post like this.

A Home to a Cat's Taste

It isn't difficult to arrange an apartment or house to suit a cat's taste. Nor does it cost much money nor do you have to set aside your own decorating ideas in order to offer your new roommate what it needs to feel comfortable.

Division of Territory

To the cat, your house or apartment is just as much a territory as outdoors in the wild. As soon as your pet has gotten to feel at home, the cat regards the place as its own personal kingdom, and the befriended human is good-naturedly allowed to share it. The cat chooses several secure resting places for itself, which preferably it alone "owns." Among them is one place that the cat inhabits in the strict sense of the word. It is the place where it feels most secure, usually a particular room, but it may be merely a preferred spot where your pet passes many hours of the day. Nina, a very dainty cat, has found just the right little spot near the small heater in the kitchen, whereas Matilda prefers to hop up on the kitchen cupboard. She has a good view from there.

Space Requirements

A one-room apartment can be as interesting for a cat as the largest house. From the cat's point of view, it's variety that provides excitement, though of course hazards should be removed (see page 22). A room where the cat can observe everything that's happening without moving from one spot becomes boring in the long run. To offer as much variety, exercise, excitement, and freedom as possible, the indoor environment should be made similar to the natural outdoor environment.

The one-room apartment: With a little imagination, a studio apartment can be arranged to provide interesting, attractive hiding places and recesses. Increase your cat's usable area by using wall space, for example, on cupboards, bookshelves, and climbing trees. Cats also love to look out of windows. It's like television for your pet. Secure spots by the windows and balcony (if there is one) can be made available easily (see page 19).

The multi-room dwelling: Several rooms make life more entertaining, for your cat, the kitchen and bathroom among them. They can be investigated over and over. The cat feels the need to make the rounds through its territory countless times a day. This inspection tour is repeated at short intervals, so the cat feels frustrated when it's impeded by doors. Insistently mewing, your pet sits in front of the door, and if it doesn't open immediately, the cat scratches at the door which leaves unsightly marks. So leave the doors open.

Furthermore, the cat certainly has nothing against a few wicker cat beds here and there from which it can see the lay of the land without being seen itself.

Arranging your home for a cat's pleasure isn't very complicated. An empty spot on a chest or cabinet provides a good lookout, a few shelves permit exciting climbing excursions, and the windowsill offers interesting opportunities for observation.

Arranging Your Home for a Cat

Litter box (1): In this sample apartment, the litter box is in the bathroom. Usually it's dark, private, and quiet, and the cat likes that. Don't forget to leave the door open.

Scratching equipment: If you don't want a cat tree or post (6) standing around in your home (it doesn't necessarily suit everyone's taste), you can attach a piece of carpet to the hall closet (2), for example. Then kitty can attack that. Naturally it's important for the scratching equipment to be located where the cat ordinarily passes it.

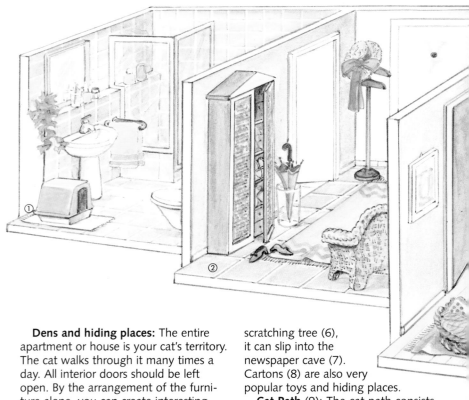

Dens and hiding places: The entire apartment or house is your cat's territory. The cat walks through it many times a day. All interior doors should be left open. By the arrangement of the furniture alone, you can create interesting and attractive hiding places and niches. Orient the sofa in the living room so that a hiding place is created behind it (3). In the kitchen, kitty cuts through, over, or under the hanging shelves (4). Your pet can creep into the cubbyhole (5) in the scratching tree (6), it can slip into the newspaper cave (7). Cartons (8) are also very popular toys and hiding places.

Cat Path (9): The cat path consists of shelving that you have upholstered with carpeting and mounted under the ceiling. To climb up, your pet needs a ladder (10). You can also utilize a cupboard for this, which you may even carpet as well. Fasten wire ladders firmly.

Climbing and Balancing: Ladders (10) and climbing trees (6) offer the cat wonderful chances to climb. A thick hemp rope (11) stretched between the climbing tree and the wall invites balancing. Also kitty loves to make use of a room-dividing element like the horizontal beam between living room and bedroom (12). It should be rectangular.

Balcony Observation Spot (13): A shelf at the height of the balcony railing takes care of this completely. The balcony must of course be secured with screening (see page 19).

Scratching and Climbing Equipment

Some kind of provision for scratching is essential in the cat-friendly home. The cat needs this equipment for several reasons. It sharpens its claws, thus exercising its extending and withdrawing reflexes; it exhibits its superiority; it works off frustration and anger, and it marks its territory. You see how impor-

Kittens play tirelessly and take special delight in equipment, such as this wooden seesaw, that allows them to outwit each other. It's easy to build one.

tant this piece of equipment is; otherwise kitty will "lay hands" on your furniture. You can buy this piece of equipment or, if you're handy, you can make one for yourself.

Making your own: The supporting column, a round or rectangular post (available in lumberyards or garden centers) is covered with sturdy carpeting (it needn't always be hemp rope). A large log is closer to nature, with the bark left on, if possible. Fasten it to the floor and wall or ceiling with angle irons so that the tree stands firm. Wood shelves, at various heights and covered with carpeting, invite sitting. Stretch a

thick rope on which the cat can balance or climb; suspend balls of wadded paper, pieces of leather, and short pieces of colored ribbons or rubber bands. Any store-bought climbing tree can also be made more interesting with such things.

Location: Place the equipment where the cat passes on its morning jaunt to its grooming spot or feeding dish. While your pet scratches on the post, the cat is also refreshing its scent-marking signs. It actually has scent glands on the pads of its front feet that rub on the tree during scratching. And if your pet lives with another cat that has had access to the tree in the meantime, your pet will immediately get down to work in order to mark its scent over the other one.

A scratching post mounted firmly to the wall or a simple hemp rug with a slip-proof backing is also suitable. In my house it's lying in the hallway, because my cats pass it there on the way from their sleeping places to their feeding place—even if there weren't also a small upholstered stool there on which I sit while using the telephone. Obviously it's my scent clinging to it that keeps provoking Nina's bad habit of adding her scent by scratching.

Sleeping Places

Be it a fancy cat bed or cardboard box, it's all the same to the cat. The main thing is that it's in a warm place. And it doesn't necessarily follow that kitty will now actually spend nights there either. It's the place under the bed covers that magically attracts the former cave dweller, and besides: What's nicer than spending the night curled up next to your pet's person? To wean your pet away from this, you have to be even more obstinate than the cat when the time comes.

In any case, in a home geared to a cat's taste you must make sure that your four-legged friend will find a cave like that somewhere or other—high up if possible, for instance in a climbing tree or on a cupboard shelf.

Litter Box

Cats bury their excrement, not so much out of cleanliness but as a sign of their rank within the cat community. Dominant, free-roaming cats leave their feces uncovered in the most conspicuous places possible as a "scent threat." On the other hand, friendly or subordinate cats bury theirs. Therefore, they also do this in a home that they share with humans, assuming it is harmonious and undisturbed. To keep it that way, you must fulfill a few requirements.

Placement: Place the litter box in a quiet, protected spot, where the cat can have privacy, for instance in the bathroom. Under no circumstances place near the feeding dishes, as this would interfere with eating. Kitty must always have access to the litter box because any upset or irritation may be a stimulus for eliminating its wastes.

Keeping it clean: Fill the box with cat litter at least two inches (2.5 to 5 cm) deep. Remove feces and damp litter every day and put in some new litter (see cat litter, page 19). Once a week put all the litter in a plastic bag and put it in the trash. Never put it in the toilet. Rinse out the litter box with hot water, but don't use any dishwashing detergent or disinfectants. Wipe dry and fill with fresh litter.

Cats are extremely fastidious and respond to any unrest or diminished cleanliness by express mail, so to speak. In protest, my Matilda will regularly urinate on clean, white places—on fresh washed laundry or, as a youngster, on a carton of envelopes.

Exercise on the Porch or Balcony

An indoor cat whose territory includes a balcony or screened porch can consider itself lucky. Your pet has access to air and sun as well as the chance to occupy various observation posts with a changing "program" according to its whim and mood. This makes for even more variety and amusement in your cat's life. However your pet must always have access to shade and must be able to go back indoors when it wishes.

Consider the following:
• Securing the balcony. To make sure the cat doesn't accidentally fall from the balcony, you must secure the balcony with screening, a fine nylon net, chicken wire, or other materials. This protects the cat and doesn't "bar" the view for you. There are landlords who don't allow enclosure, so ask about this ahead of time.

As well as considering the danger of falling, bear in mind that there will be trouble with the neighbors if the cat walks over the roof and gets into strangers' apartments.
• Furnishing the balcony or porch. Depending on the situation, you can erect a natural scratching and climbing tree with lookout platforms. Provide for one or two resting places between the flower boxes.

Also consider having a planter with cat grass so that kitty won't be tempted to eat your plants (see How to Make the Home Safe for Cats, page 22)

Cats stroll through their territory—in this case, the apartment or house—countless times a day. Therefore, except for outside doors, no doors should be left closed; otherwise, in the attempt to open them, the cats will leave unattractive scratch marks.

Typical Cats

Even indoors, the cat exhibits instinctual behavior patterns and habits. Learn to interpret them to better understand your cat.

The game of quarry with a fur mouse.

Claw sharpening is pursued with zeal.

Photo left: Wool yarn is interesting because of its softness and the yarn-tangling game.

Photo, right: Completely relaxed despite full tension— only a cat can lie there like this.

Drinking milk out of a narrow glass…

is no problem for a cat.

How to Make the Home Safe for Cats

Sources of Danger	Possible Results	Avoiding the Danger
Balconies and open windows	Danger of falling	Secure with wire or nylon netting.
Opened tilting windows	While jumping through the crack, the cat can get caught and strangle.	Secure with special inserts.
"Caves" such as open cupboards and drawers, clothes dryers and dishwashers, floor vases, plastic bags, small cracks and holes	All dark holes magically lure cats and they can become wedged or they can suffocate (see drawing below).	Check before closing drawers and cupboard doors or before starting machines (also microwaves and freezers). Cover empty vases, cover cracks behind and under furniture.
Doors that cats can open by jumping on the handles (French doors)	In the case of the apartment door, this can lead to unpleasant surprises.	Fix the handle with a stick or wedge, or always keep the door locked.
Hot burners, open pans and pots in which there is food frying and liquid boiling, alcohol lamps, an iron, candles, and burning cigarettes	Curious cats can burn their feet.	Before leaving the kitchen, cover pots and pans or place a covered pot of water on top of a hot stove burner. Turn off the iron, blow out alcohol lamps and candles, don't leave burning cigarettes and butts lying around.
Needles and pins	Cats can walk on them or swallow them.	Don't leave anything lying around.
Washing and cleaning agents, chemicals, pills	Poisoning	Everything that's dangerous for children is also dangerous for kittens and cats so lock it all away.
Plants, including cyclamen, azalea, dieffenbachia (dumb cane), ivy, hyacinth, philodendron, primula (primrose), and poinsettia. See the complete list of poisonous plants, pages 60.	Poisoning	In general, cats are so discriminating that they only nibble on nonpoisonous plants; but you should keep inexperienced cats away from poisonous plants.

"Caves" like the drum of a clothes dryer magically attract cats, so it's best to check before closing doors.

A Cat Arrives at Your House

Finally it's happened. You can get the cat. The transport cage—it should be a plastic pet carrier or kennel—has already been prepared for this moment. Take the car, and take a friend, too. Then one of you can talk reassuringly to the cat during the trip. When you get home, put the carrier in its place and open it up.

Acclimating the Young Cat

It's best if you give the kitten the run of only one room at first (in a one-room apartment this naturally takes care of itself). Put the litter box in the room with it and also a small saucer of the food the kitten is accustomed to (find out from the previous owner), and a saucer of water. Crouch down beside the carrier and coax the little animal out by gently calling its name. Certainly it will be meowing for its mother and siblings. Answer it with a gentle voice so that it can get used to you. Soon the kitten will curiously venture out and take a look at its new home. At first your pet will slink along the walls and hide under the couch, chairs, and cupboards, and it may even be impossible to lure the kitten out from under there. Wait patiently nearby and eventually the kitten will approach you.

The young cat's bond to its mother and siblings is very strong. You must replace the loss for the kitten, stroke it, scratch it, and play with it. Always be prepared for the kitten to run trustingly between your legs and rub up against you with its little head, or try to climb up your leg. The kitten also has no inkling that a slammed door can be life threatening; therefore, always look around carefully before closing doors. Also, such a tiny creature can get itself into impossible situations. So you must keep a close eye on your pet.

Acclimating the Older Cat

In theory, the acclimation for an older cat doesn't go any differently than for a young cat. Still, because the cat is accustomed its old environment, you must take that into consideration and help the cat adapt to the new environment.

The anxious cat: Your may have had bad experiences with people. Try to find out what it's afraid of. This could be movements, sounds, or a lot of commotion or confusion in the household. Perhaps you already have another pet—a dog, a parrot, or another cat—that your new pet is afraid of. Don't use any pressure, and always provide a hiding place for the cat to withdraw into. Your pet needs a quiet environment and should not be frightened by abrupt advances. That will only make the cat more afraid.

The difficult cat: You've gotten your pet from a shelter and now it scratches and bites when you want to touch it. Only love and patience will help that. Don't grab the cat. Give it cat food regularly, and be quiet and relaxed around it. Gradually your pet will get to know you and you'll earn its trust.

It's also difficult for a cat after many years of living with one person to get

A kitten that has just been separated from its mother and siblings needs much understanding and affection when it arrives at its new home. Try not to leave the little creature alone for the first few hours and days.

The cat uses the ladder to reach a high lookout spot.

regard the home as its own personal domain and defend it against newcomers of the same species (see Cats and Other Cats, page 12). The cat wants nothing to do with the intruder, even if it's a young kitten. Nevertheless, kittens have the uninhibitedness of youth, and you should make use of that in the getting-acquainted period. Let the new kitten explore at first. While this is going on, sit with the old cat on your lap in your usual chair, stroking it and talking reassuringly to your pet. That has a calming effect, and perhaps the cat will even begin to purr. This is a reassuring sound to the newcomer, which it certainly will investigate. When the old cat allows the new one to make nose contact, a first step has been taken. Also, a small kitten usually isn't scared away very quickly by a hiss or a swipe of a paw. Unconcerned, it will run along behind the big one, imitating what it does and inviting it to play by romping and swiping at its tail. In time, the old cat won't be able to resist this bundle of charm, anthropomorphically speaking, and will learn to value the variety and entertainment that the kitten has added to its life.

Obviously, each animal should have its own food dish and, if possible, also its own litter box, not to mention a sleeping place of its own, which the cat has chosen at its own discretion, so to speak, and will also defend.

Cats and Dogs

Young dog: If both the dog and cat are young, you hardly need to interfere. Because both are much too curious and unconcerned to annoy the other, they each playfully and independently learn each other's language, (see Cats and Other Household Pets, page 13). Thus, they can live in peace and become friends.

used to a new one. The cat may have been so close to its former master or mistress that it now feels almost overwhelmed with homesickness and grief.

Old Cats and New Arrivals

When my Burmese cat Nina lost her companion, she acted very sad and forlorn, so we decided to get her a companion again by getting a kitten. It was clear that it wasn't going to be love at first sight. It's in the nature of the cat to

Adult dog: You can get a well-trained dog to take the kitten into its pack if you do the following:

• Keep the two of them separated until the kitten has made the first exploratory round of the new environment.

• Let the dog in, and give it the command "Sit." If it's very temperamental, put the dog on the lead so it can't run after the kitten. The kitten will then curiously approach it, but flee at once as soon as the dog moves.

• Make certain that the dog doesn't injure or terrorize the kitten. Everything else will take its course, and soon the dog will play its role as protector of the new arrival as well.

A real friendship may arise between the two of them. When my cat Meow-Meow would steal something from the table, she always gave the patiently waiting dog Willy something too. Perhaps she just wanted to make sure he wouldn't bark.

Cats and Children

If the kitten is still young, you should show your child how to pick the pet up properly and carry it, how to stroke it—with the lay of the fur, not against the grain—and how to play with it (see HOW-TO: Playing, page 38). Emphasize to your child that the kitten must not be bathed because it's not good for it. An adult cat can defend itself against too vigorous expressions of love. It simply goes away or hisses and shows its claws. Cats require a good deal of care and you can't expect your child to take all the responsibility for the cat. You must keep an eye out for the cat and make sure your child knows how to feed and groom it. However, you should never leave a cat alone with a sleeping baby. The cat can lie on the child's chest and head—with tragic consequences.

From there, the cat trail continues across cupboards and bookshelves.

What the Cat Should Learn

As a rule, the education of a young cat isn't a big problem. It has just left its mother and has learned from her through example and imitation.

In fact, by the time you get your pet—as a rule around 10 to 12 weeks old—the kitten has already developed some behavior patterns that cannot be changed. Unlike dogs, cats have finished the socialization phase by this time. Bad habits cannot be eliminated, wrong imprinting cannot be changed. One can therefore paraphrase the proverb and

HOW-TO:
The Health Checkup

How You Can Recognize a Healthy Cat

When you look for a young kitten, don't look only for a sweet appearance but also look for good condition and temperament. Healthy kittens play and tumble about a great deal. In between their periods of play they stop to rest, often without any transition from their vigorous romping. They are, of course, cautious with unfamiliar people but still interested and curious. Sick kittens, on the other hand, sit around passively, and may act apathetic and disinterested in the action around them. What you need to observe in detail is described below:

• The coat feels thick and soft, never shaggy, however, the baby coat won't be as smooth and shining as the coat of an adult cat.
• The eyes are clear and shining; they should display neither tears nor any other abnormality.
• The nose is dry and warm but not hot.
• The ears react to all the sounds of the environment and are clean inside. Shaking and/or holding the head on one side indicates an ear inflammation.
• The anal region must be clean. Dirt and fur clumped together with feces indicate diarrhea.
• The belly should not appear fat or bloated, except right after eating, because many kittens eat until their tummies bulge.

• The kitten's body should feel well "upholstered" and solid, and should not feel light as a feather when you pick it up.

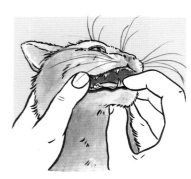

1] Inspect your cat's teeth regularly for tartar buildup.

Regular Examinations

Cats have the reputation for being tougher and more hardy and disease resistant than other animals. You can help them maintain this natural resistance by carrying out the following examination from time to time. But don't forget that the most successful way to keep your cat healthy is through proper maintenance and care (see page 40). For the animal this means that it is able to live just exactly as is appropriate to its species. however, if the cat ever sits around listless and bored, it isn't necessarily an immediate indication of a health problem.

Teeth Inspection
Drawing 1

About three weeks after birth the kitten gets its milk teeth, which are replaced at about 5 months by the permanent teeth.

The change of teeth occurs almost unnoticed, because the milk teeth are either spit out or swallowed. The set of milk teeth consists of 26 teeth, and the permanent set consists of 30.

Tartar buildup: In cats, tartar buildup is promoted by eating canned or soft cat food. You can help prevent this by giving your cat both canned and crunchy, dry food. Dry cat food acts as a mini "toothbrush." If your cat has a persistent problem with tartar buildup or gingivitis, ask your veterinarian to teach you how to brush your cat's teeth. Tartar should be removed by the veterinarian.

Gum inflammation: (Gingivitis) This often arises from tartar buildup or from infections in the mouth and jaw. Some breeds are also prone to gingivitis. You can recognize it by a red line on the gums near the teeth, and the bad smell of the cat's breath.

Inspection of Anal Region
Drawing 2

Residues of fecal material at the anus indicate diarrhea, which can have numerous causes, for example, intestinal upset from improper feeding, intestinal parasites, or viral diseases. Therefore, diarrhea is always an alarm signal, particularly if it continues for a long time, (see Illness: Prevention and Care, page 46). Take your cat to the veterinarian for a thorough checkup.

The dirty anal region is cleaned with a damp cloth.

Inspection of the Skin

Skin diseases develop very quickly in cats. Cats should therefore have regular skin inspections in order to nip a potential illness in the bud. This is also important for you, because some skin infections are communicable to

2] A stained anal region, can indicate diarrhea.

human beings (see page 47). If you notice any changes in your cat's skin, take the cat to the veterinarian as soon as possible.

A clear indication that something is wrong with the cat's skin is constant scratching in a particular spot.

Fungus diseases of the skin: Ringworm is recognizable, by round, bare places, which sometimes develop into heavily crusted or scaly spots. The hairs at these spots break or often fall out. Usually the itching isn't very severe. Because ringworm can be passed to humans, take your cat to the veterinarian as soon as possible.

Parasites, such as fleas, can be recognized by inflamed places in the skin and falling hair.

However, these symptoms can also occur from allergies or hormonal disturbances as well. All

these diseases can only be correctly diagnosed and appropriately treated by the veterinarian.

Inspection of the Ears
Drawing 3

Cats' ears can be attacked internally by ear mites and, externally by skin infections, resulting in inflammation. With regular inspection of your cat, such diseases can be recognized in time and treated at once so they don't get worse. Warning signs are constant head shaking and scratching at the ear. Smeary deposits and brown crusts inside the ear indicate ear mites; very red and inflamed skin in the auditory canal (illuminated with a pocket flashlight) is a sign of ear inflammation; small bald spots on the ears indicate a skin disease.

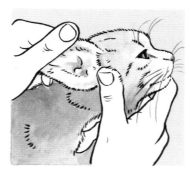

3] Ear inspection allows any ear mite infestation to be recognized early.

As soon as you notice any of the above signs of disease in your cat, you should take your cat to the veterinarian as soon as possible.

Inspection of the Eyes

A cat's eyes are normally clean and clear. If the eyelid is inflamed, the eyes can be red and sensitive to touch, have a gummy yellow discharge, and the nictitating eyelid may slide up from the lower lid and corner of the eye near the nose, appearing as a whitish pink layer of skin over the eyeball.

Sometimes foreign bodies get into the eye, for example, a small hair, a fiber, a grain of sand. Symptoms of this are sudden, abundant flow of tears from one eye. If the foreign body, has burrowed into the outer surface of the eye, it causes great pain. Even if you can see it, you should let a veterinarian remove it, because you could seriously damage the eye. Persian cats need special attention. Their huge eyes, narrow tear ducts, and short noses ("stops") cause constant tearing. Unfortunately even the veterinarian can't do anything for these conditions, which are a result of the breeding practices used by breeders. Here the only help is daily cleaning with a dampened soft tissue or cotton balls. (see HOW-TO: Grooming, page 34).

say, what a kitten hasn't learned, the cat will never learn. For example, if a kitten hasn't had any contact with human beings during the socialization phases, it will always be shy in their presence later. This sensitive phase embraces more or less the first two to seven weeks of life, although neither the beginning nor the end of the period is established exactly. Some kittens that are older than seven weeks can still get used to people, even if with considerably more difficulty. In any case, it's better if the kitten is raised by a mother cat who trusts "her" people, for she conveys this to her young. This is also a reason why you should have a good look around before buying a cat from a breeder or cat owner, and should pay attention to such details (see How You Get a Cat, page 10). If it turns out the kitten you have chosen is well socialized, you only have to reinforce this training in the right way and manner (see HOW-TO: Training, page 30).

Before it becomes a cat, a kitten should learn that not everything is allowed.

• The cat has already learned to use the litter box and cover its feces/wastes. It is important to therefore reinforce this behavior when you get your pet home.
• Scratching is part of a cat's instinctual, normal behavior. It is best to place the scratching equipment in the right spot and regularly practice with the kitten.
• Sleeping on the bed, jumping on the table, climbing the curtains, or begging at meals are bad feline habits. These should be countered with consistent correction.

Neutering

You won't be able to avoid neutering if you are going to keep your cat indoors. Many cat owners are reluctant to neuter on the principle that it only serves the interest of humans. If you should happen to think so too, realize that you must deal with the constant marking behavior of the tomcat on your well-cared-for furniture or with the insistent yowls of the female cat almost constantly in heat, which robs you of your nightly rest. (See Male or Female?, page 11.) The operation is always performed by a veterinarian and under anesthesia. Usually the cat can be brought home again the same day or the day after.

Tomcat: After he achieves sexual maturity—between the sixth and ninth months—the tomcat's testicles are removed. Because of the anesthetic, you mustn't feed him the evening before the operation. As a rule, he's back on his feet again very quickly.

Neutered tomcats that live alone sometimes tend to overeat and then become overweight. Only two things will help that: more activity and less food.

Female: Female cats can be spayed at six to nine months, and should be spayed before their first heat (studies have shown that cats spayed before their first heat have a lower incidence of tumors). The ovaries and usually a portion of the uterus are removed. The incision is closed with sutures, which are either removed later by the veterinarian, or if "dissolving" sutures are used, will dissolve on their own. When your pet is released to your care (the night of the operation or the next day), let it sleep in a warm, quiet spot, and make sure that she doesn't do any acrobatics for the first week. In case of complications, such as redness, swelling, or excessive licking of the sutures and incision area, consult your veterinarian.

Sterilization: This procedure only makes the male and female sterile. The spermatic ducts or oviducts are severed, the sex drive is retained, and therefore the annoying behaviors are not removed.

No, kitty! It is best to train your pet early not to jump on the table and nibble plants.

The pill: Recommended only for breeding cats, who aren't supposed to come into heat until the right time, the pill if given over a long period, can damage the uterus and the liver, causing diabetes.

HOW-TO:
Training

Cats have their own ideas and can't be forced to do anything. The kitten learns by imitation; it observes its mother and copies what she does. Now you must take over this role. Setting an example is the only practical way of training young cats. On the other hand, with the adult cat, who has lived according to its own laws for a long time, training consists of establishing limitations, and using positive reinforcement so that the cat stops its undesirable behavior.

Five Training Rules
1. Always speak quietly to the cat. Only when your pet trusts you will it do what you want.
2. Always use consistent reinforcement. Don't stop the cat from begging at the table today and then feed your pet tomorrow.
3. Don't scream. Utter a decided "No!" when your pet scratches at the armchair again and not the scratching post, for example. However, never say the name of the cat loudly to stop it.
4. Be consistent. Always use the same expressions, such as "No!" "Down!" or "Out!"
5. Always praise or reproach immediately. Stroke or praise the cat when it has obeyed you. Scold your pet firmly and clearly with words, or if need be with a light tap with a folded newspaper, but only if you catch the cat in the act.

1] Practice with your cat sharpening its claws on the scratching tree, post, or rug.

Housebreaking
As a rule a kitten is housebroken when you receive it. Sometime after the third week of life, it begins to use the litter box. The kitten has imitated its mother, for she is now no longer helping it urinate and defecate. Now it's up to you to accustom your kitten to the new location of the litter box. If you notice that the kitten has to go, quickly place your pet in the box. It helps to be observant. Usually the kitten will meow, look around, and scratch at the floor, before it squats with its tail lifted and does its business. Afterward praise and stroke your kitten. Ordinarily, housebreaking succeeds immediately. But there are also animals that need a little more help. You should watch such a cat very carefully and try to catch it at the right moment.

2] Climbing on the curtains can be prevented with a sudden squirt from the plant sprayer.

Praise your pet a lot each time it goes into the box. You should also scold the kitten, but only when you catch it at the time.

Sharpening Claws
Drawing 1
The cat must learn not to sharpen its claws on the furniture or rugs but only on the scratching equipment provided for your pet. Whether that is a scratching tree, post, or rug doesn't matter. As soon as you see that the cat is beginning to scratch on the chair or carpet, take your pet to the scratching equipment. Place the post where the cat will pass on the path between its sleeping place or usual resting place and the feeding dish. Show your pet how it can scratch its claws on it by placing its paws on the equipment and moving them. Repeat this a few times until the cat has got the idea.

Begging at the Table
A cat that constantly begs while you are eating is a pain. To break the habit, you should use consistent reinforcement.

- Put a little food in its dish when you sit down to eat.
- Prevent your pet from approaching with a firm "No" when the cat moves in the direction of your table.
- If the cat jumps into your lap during the meal, set the cat on the floor with the command "Down!"
- Under no circumstances throw or give anything to the cat, even once. If you do, all the earlier measures are in vain.

Breaking Bad Habits
Drawings 2, 3, and 4

Squirt bottles, bellows (that force air through a nozzle), water pistols, or small aluminum chains are all things that can serve to discourage the animal. If your cat climbs up the curtains, scratches its claws on your best chair, or jumps on the kitchen table where you've placed your groceries, a surprising stream of water or air helps deter stubborn repeat offenders. Make sure you catch the cat in the act and send the stream of water, chain or air at the cat wordlessly. You shouldn't be associated with the correction and connect the

4] Frightened by the tossed aluminum chain, the cat stops scratching the armchair.

"inhibiting stimulus" to yourself. It's even more successful, using the aluminum chain, for example, if you can always manage to toss it at the beginning of the undesired activity.

Walking on a Lead

Cats are not like dogs that you can lead on a leash and expect to heel. It's another matter to get cats accustomed to a leash, which in some cases can be useful, such as when you go to the veterinarian (see page 48).

Most practical is the cat halter, which goes around the chest and belly (available in the pet supply store). This is how you get the cat to adapt to it:

Getting used to the lead: Let the cat play with the leash for several days.

Putting on the halter: At first let the cat wear the halter for a short time, then for longer and longer periods. Let the cat play with it before putting it on.

Getting used to walking: Put on the harness, attach the lead, and lure the cat with a toy so that it stretches the lead and gets used to the feeling. Praise and stroke your pet when it does well.

Walking on the lead: Lure the cat with a treat so that it moves forward. Don't forget to praise and stroke your pet. Finally lead the cat around the apartment until she goes without resistance. Now kitty is ready for the first outing.

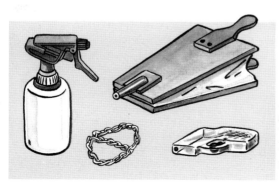

3] Spray bottles, bellows, or water pistols used as an "inhibiting stimulus" spoil the misdeed for the cat.

Living With a Cat

What You Must Do for the Cat

Matilda had slept for many hours in her favorite place under the sofa cover. But then she was there, slipping around my legs, rubbing against my chair, and demanding her tribute of stroking. The indoor cat seems to bond more closely to its people and also very clearly shows its affections.

In living with a cat, therefore, it isn't just a matter of the necessities like a scratching post and a litter box. (see All the Things a Cat Needs, page 14). Within your four walls, besides its regular meals and just as much, kitty needs you to spend time together: petting, playing, cuddling, and then more of the same. Young kittens, especially, always want to be picked up over and over again and to feel your affection. And if you just absolutely don't have time at the moment, you should at least talk to them in a friendly way.

Stroking, playing, and cuddling should be part of the daily routine of an apartment cat— not only when it's small and cute.

What You Can Expect from the Cat

The cat lives by us, with us, but not for us, someone said once. You should respect this in your joint life with your velvet-pawed housemate. As long as your cat is sleeping or resting or going its own secret way, it doesn't want to be bothered. Taking your pet in your arms or trying to play at such moments is utterly wrong. The cat won't react at all, or only unwillingly, and possibly may even scratch and bite. However, if it's your pet's own idea, the cat will give you no peace until you do whatever your pet has in mind.

Indoor cats far more often meet visitors and strangers than cats that go outside a great deal. However, you can't expect them to be trustful of all strangers on that account. Nina remains quietly lying in her spot, whereas Matilda only shows herself again when there's no longer anyone there.

Should You Declaw Your Cat?

Declawing of domestic cats is highly controversial in this country. Some countries, such as Britain, have outlawed the practice altogether. Many breeders, veterinarians, cat registries, and cat associations feel that cats should not be declawed under any circumstances. Others think it's acceptable, depending on the circumstances.

The American Veterinary Medical Association's position on declawing is "declawing of domestic cats is justifiable when the cat cannot be trained to refrain from using its claws destructively."

Before contemplating this surgery, consider the following:

• Declawing removes the germinal cells and some or all of the terminal bone in the toe, similar to removing a human's fingers at the first joint. The surgery is irreversible.

• The surgery is done under general anesthesia and the cat is subject to all the risks that surgery entails.

• Declawing removes your cat's ability to defend itself and to climb to

Kitty has chosen the wing chair as her favorite place. From here she can observe everything.

avoid attackers; declawed cats therefore should not be allowed outside.

• Declawed cats cannot be shown in cat shows.

• Some cat owners say they have noticed personality changes in their cats, including failure to use the litter box appropriately, after the surgery was performed.

Because cats can be trained to use a scratching post appropriately, make every effort to teach a cat proper scratching behavior before resorting to surgical alteration.

Another option to consider is a product called Soft Paws Nail Caps for cats. These soft vinyl caps are applied over the cat's trimmed nails and held in place with a small amount of adhesive, effectively blunting the claws and making it impossible for the cat to cause damage to your furniture. The caps last until the nail grows out, approximately four to eight weeks. The first application is done by your veterinarian, who also trains you in the application process at the same time. From then on, you can do the application yourself at home.

HOW-TO:
Grooming

The cat grooms its fur thoroughly many times a day. The much-noted cat bath is actually a basic drive. However, human help is still necessary, especially the grooming of long-haired cats.

Coat Care
Drawing 1

Short-haired and semi-long-haired cats must only be brushed daily during the shedding season so they don't swallow too much fur when the groom themselves and vomit up the hair balls that form in their stomachs. But brushing also means attention and is enjoyed by most cats, and they reward you by purring loudly. When you groom the coat with a rubber curry brush, you're also massaging your cat along with it. Brush from neck to tail, with the grain, and then firmly stroke the fur with a slightly dampened rubber glove. Being brushed against the grain is uncomfortable for the cat.

Washing and Combing

Only a long-haired cat whose coat is very dirty has to be bathed. The basin or pan should be large enough so that there's just enough room for the cat in it, like a handwashing basin or a large bucket. Use a specially formulated cat flea shampoo (obtainable in pet supply stores), which is effective against fleas and ticks. Be sure to use one that says "safe for cats." Let lukewarm water run into the basin, hold the cat by the front paws with one hand, wash with the other. Never dunk the head. Carefully rinse out the shampoo and then rub the animal down afterward with a prewarmed towel. For combing, take the cat on your lap. With a wide-tooth metal comb, comb out the undercoat, especially thoroughly on the belly and between the legs. Keep talking soothingly to the cat while you are doing it, and never use force. Then comb with the fine-tooth comb. The coat can dry in a warm room by itself. It's faster with a hair dryer, but it causes the fur to become dull. A drying brush is most comfortable for the cat, and besides the coat shines as well.

1] Coat care with a rubber curry brush is ideal. It enables kitty to receive a beneficial massage at the same time.

Brushing and Powdering
Drawing 2

The coat of the long-haired cat that has been previously combed gets its silky shine back with brushing. A natural-bristle brush is best for this. You can brush out the problem areas on the belly and in the chest region well with these, too, holding the cat's front paws up. About once a month, the coat can be cleaned with powder (available in the pet supply store). Use it sparingly, because it dries out the skin. Rub the powder in, let it work overnight, and the next day brush out thoroughly, even against the grain as well.

If your cat gets used to the procedure from the beginning, your pet won't develop fear and rejection. Some cats defend themselves vehemently against it. Try to alternate brushing and

2] A slightly dirty coat can be cleaned once a month with a special powder. Let the powder stay on overnight, then brush it out thoroughly the next day.

stroking. In most instances, this has a calming effect.

Removing Snarls
Drawing 3

First divide a knot in the fur with your fingers and then try to untangle it with a steel comb. If this doesn't work, cut out the knot with a seam-ripping tool or a "snarl breaker" tool found at pet supply stores. Direct the point of the tool with your finger so as not to injure the animal's skin.

Important note: Persians that are not combed and brushed regularly and whose fur tangles because of it are very unhappy. Often they will pull out their fur in patches, won't eat, and experience great pain. A great many must be shorn by the veterinarian under anesthesia.

Cleaning Eyes
Drawing 4

Remove light deposits in the corners of the eyes with a dampened, soft facial tissue or cotton ball. Always wipe from the outer corner of the eye to the inner corner. Sudden, abundant tear-

ing from one eye can indicate a foreign body in the eye. Only the veterinarian can remove the foreign body. Persian cats, especially, with their indented nose ("stop") often have a narrowing or obstruction of the tear ducts and therefore have tearing eyes that leave yellow stains on the face. The eyes must be dried several times daily with a clean, soft facial tissue or cotton ball. The veterinarian can also prescribe eye drops.

3] Divide fur tangles into smaller bunches with your fingers and then comb out the snarls with a steel comb or use a seam-ripping tool.

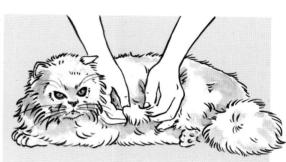

Ear Care

The ears should also be inspected regularly. If necessary, carefully remove dirt from the ear with a tissue.

Caution: Never use a cotton-tipped swab for cleaning and never enter the ear canal. If little dark clumps are visible and the cat is scratching frequently and shaking its head, this indicates ear mites (see HOW-TO: The Health Checkup, page 26). Take your cat to the veterinarian.

Claw Care

Indoor cats often don't wear down their claws enough, so they become too curved or curled under. You should regularly clip them with a special clipper (available from the pet supply store). Only cut the transparent part of the claw, which has no blood vessels, or you'll injure the cat.

Note: Sometimes on or around the scratching equipment you will find something that looks like a

torn-out claw. This is only the external layer of claw that has been shed in the scratching process, revealing the shiny new claw underneath.

4] Remove encrustations in the corners of the eyes and tear ducts with a dampened facial tissue or cotton ball.

This is a positive and painless alternative to declawing, and is safe for your cat, because the nail tips are harmless if swallowed. They even come in several decorator colors! See your veterinarian for more information.

Vacation—Where Can You Take a Cat?

The widespread idea that cats are loners and don't suffer when they're left alone is false—in the case of the indoor cat particularly. It's true that they feel best in their own familiar environment, but they don't want to be without the presence of people. You should take this into consideration with the question of what to do with the cat while you are on vacation. Various solutions can be considered.

Leaving the cat at home: For this you need a reliable person who can come once or twice daily to feed the cat, and clean the litter pan, and who also has enough time to cuddle and play with kitty.

Unconcerned, the kitten explores its new environment.

Taking the cat with you: If you accustom your cat to traveling when it is young, you can also take your pet with you. A constantly changing vacation spot would cause too great a stress for the animal, however. But if you always go to the same vacation house, your cat would love to go with you.

Boarding: If you do not have friends with whom the cat feels comfortable, boarding is easier on your cat, and less stressful. You should inspect a boarding cattery carefully beforehand. The animal will be required to have all its immunization shots (see page 46).

Traveling with a Cat

Getting Used to the Car

A few days beforehand, set out the cat carrier so that kitty can make friends. Once you've placed your pet inside and it's made itself comfortable, carry the cat in the carrier, talking comfortingly, and put the cat in the car. Then bring your pet back inside. Its confidence will be strengthened this way. The next time drive a short distance with the cat, and if it handles this stress without any reaction of fear, there won't be any more great difficulties.

Before the trip: If it's going to be a long trip, you shouldn't give the cat anything to eat during the journey or the night before so that its stomach will be empty.

During the trip: In any case, you should have a plastic box with cat litter available. There should be a dish of water, too, though the cat will only drink sparingly, even when it's terribly hot. Only let the animal out of the carrier in the car if the cat will sit quietly in its place. Be sure that you do not leave the cat in the car, even for a few minutes. On a hot day, your cat could be overcome by heat exhaustion; on a cold day, your cat could become chilled.

The cat peers over the edge of its resting place with extreme interest.

Never leave your cat in the trunk of your car.

If you are taking a long trip, be sure to check ahead of time to see if your pet will be welcome at the accommodations where you will be staying. Also check the trains, airplanes, ships that you will be using for transport on your trip, to see if pets are allowed and what regulations are imposed. Some allow you to keep your pet with you in the passenger section; I recommend you do not use transport that will only allow your pet in the baggage area.

Train travel: Cats may ride with you cost-free if you keep them in a closed basket or carrier.

Air travel: Only on some airlines are cats allowed in the cabin with you in a carrier. Check with the airline beforehand.

Note: Don't let your pet outside until it's completely at home inside the house.

How to Make Moving Easier for the Cat

Moving is stressful for people and animals. But you can soften it for your cat by helping it get used to the new territory. Even if your pet has had access to the outside before, it can get used to a new home without any outside access.
• Keep the animal in an emptied room with its familiar things (basket, litter box) until the confusion of moving is over.
• Next, drive your pet with you to the new home.
• There place your cat in a still empty room with its things again.
• After the new home is resettled, lead the cat to the new place for the litter box.
• Let your pet explore her strange new environment undisturbed.

HOW-TO:
Playing

Cats Must Play

In play, young kittens practice later behavior patterns: stalking, hiding, chasing, snatching, bit-

Balancing
Drawing 1

It's a daily occurrence for any free-roaming cat to tightrope-walk along a picket fence or a small branch. Why shouldn't your pet also be able to do it in your house or apartment? However, there must be a stimulus for the cat to go from one side to another when it's crossing

1] The cat balances on a broomstick with ease. But make sure that the broom is firmly fastened down on both ends or your pet may never try this "trick" again.

cise with the command "Jump!" But don't let your pet run under or around the hoop. The cat may only get to the other side by hopping. Only then does it receive the reward. You can teach the cat to jump through a ring formed by your arms the same way.

Hiding
Drawing 3

Nothing intrigues the former primeval cave-dwelling cat more than a dark hole, for example, a newspaper tunnel. When the paper crackles a little as well, what could that mean but a mouse in the house! Then the intrigue is doubly great. Place the (finished) newspaper folded out like a roof on the floor and let the pages rattle mysteriously. The cat won't hesitate to get to the heart of the matter.

Even an empty cardboard box is highly interesting, especially if the opening is only a crack wide. Kitty won't rest until it has forced itself

ing, and springing on the prey. While living with people, hunting is unnecessary for a cat, but the instincts remain and lie unused if the cat has nothing at its disposal to fulfill this drive. Thus, playing with your pet is a requirement for a fulfilling feline life. Included in the following suggestions are also a few tricks that you can teach your cat while playing. As has been well noted, you can't compel cats to do anything they don't want to do. But luckily cats never grow up. They love to play even when they become senior-citizen cats.

a narrow pole. In this case the stimulus is a treat. Lure the cat with a tidbit and when it balances on the broomstick, reward and praise your pet. When your cat has finally mastered the "trick," it will perform without any extra tidbits.

Jumping Through Hoops
Drawing 2

Begin by placing the hoop upright on the floor and luring the cat through it by holding a treat under its nose. But your pet doesn't get the treat until it's crossed to the other side. Gradually hold the hoop higher and higher. As soon as the cat can't walk through the hoop anymore, accompany the exer-

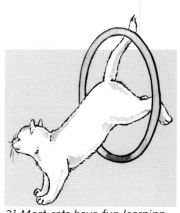

2] Most cats have fun learning tricks.

into the "cave." What's even more fun is if the second cat wants to go in after the first, because defending and occupying a territory are part of the fun.

Rolling

Empty round, plastic washing detergent buckets (the jumbo-sized kind) with the handles removed, or any large, plastic container that was not used to contain toxic materials, are good. Remove all the remains of the contents and glue carpet remnants onto the bucket/container so that kitty can also scratch its claws. The dark cave invites your cat to climb in. Your cat can also roll around in it, too, and jump on it and over it, and two cats can play hide-and-seek. When a cat is sitting inside, you can scratch on the outside a little and increase the fun.

Playing Ball

Give your cat a hard rubber ball with a graspable outer surface, big enough that the cat cannot swallow it. I advise against soft sponge-rubber balls because the cats can tear them and eat them. If the ball rolls well, the cat will chase it tirelessly as long as you keep throwing it for your pet. Furthermore, cats practice fishing with this play behavior. With a deft movement of the paw they throw the ball high over their shoulder, turn around with lightning speed, follow it, and pounce to "kill" it. It's the same as the way a cat angles after a fish. The cat runs along until the fish swims near the shore, slips its paw under the fish's body, flings the fish up

onto the grass, and then pounces on the prey.

Stalking and Chasing

My cats just love stalking and chasing. As an invitation, I crouch

3] Any kind of cave—even a roof of newspapers—invites kitty to crawl inside.

down and slap my hands on the floor. Then Nina whips around the corner. Now I creep after her. It's clear that she hears me coming. I stomp like an elephant for her, which doesn't keep her from waiting expectantly until I finally peek around the corner. She sits there quietly, big eyed, with only the tip of her tail twitching with excite-

Rolling around in an empty, well cleaned bucket is one of kitty's favorite games.

ment. The next moment she rushes away, and I must of course go after her. But, only to the nearest chair, behind which I hide. Then it's her turn to stalk the enemy. It's the same way you play with a small child—cats are, after all, like children.

Jumping High

Perhaps your cat is a talented high jumper. Some can be encouraged to regular twisting leaps. You can make the toys for your pet yourself. Fasten a rubber band to a ball of crumpled paper and whip it back and forth in front of the cat's nose. Your cat will swat at it, jump after it, and try to catch the ball that rustles so beautifully.

A Healthy Diet for Indoor Cats

You can feed your cats well-balanced meals using ready made food, whose various flavors allow you to provide variety in the cat's menu.

Both my cats often curl in the sofa corner sleeping deeply for a long time. But scarcely have I gone into the kitchen with the intention of fixing their food—it is their dinnertime—than they are rubbing around my legs with shining eyes and high-held tails.

In the course of an indoor cat's day, the mealtime assumes great importance. After all, your housemates must do without all the excitement that catching their own food would offer, which of course they have no way of knowing. So it's appropriate to use a little imagination to provide them with variety.

What the Cat Needs to Live

Cats are born mouse hunters. They wait with endless patience in front of a mouse hole until the mouse shows itself and even then they only pounce when their quarry is entirely certain. The energy necessary for this comes from the nutrients that cats receive packed in small portions in their prey: muscle tissue, liver, bones, viscera, in addition to plant and mineral materials from the stomach and intestinal contents. The building blocks of their diet are proteins, fats, carbohydrates, vitamins, and minerals. To keep the indoor cat healthy, the food it gets from you must be constituted according to its needs.

Quality, Not Quantity

Regularly feeding your cat too much makes it fat: An indoor cat doesn't need anywhere near as much energy as a mouser. That's obvious. However, if the food offered your pet is always in the form of high-calorie treats, superfluous calories is the result, and this turns into fat deposits in the cat (as with people). The question of how much to feed is therefore very important for your house cat (see HOW-TO: Feeding, page 42).

In judging how much food is enough, don't rely so much on the weight of your cat as on its physique. Small cats will become overweight faster than large ones. You should take this into account.

Get your animal accustomed to two feeding times, preferably in the morning and evening. In any case, your cat won't hesitate to remind you about it (see HOW-TO: Training, page 30).

My tip: The morning feeding time can become real drudgery on days on which you want to sleep late. Because I leave a little dry food in the dish for them to nibble, my cats leave me in peace.

Too much of one kind of food makes a cat finicky: Cats that you've accustomed to having delicacies will scarcely permit themselves to be changed to another diet. They can become greedy for certain foods, for instance, liver. Avoid a diet that is too fatty and too one-sided, give them food that is as full of variety as possible and is appropriate for cats, and respect the manner in which the cat eats.

No one is in sight! So the temptation to snatch something from the table is great.

Prepared Food

Prepared foods in boxes, bags, or cans are practical. You need simply open a can to provide a menu that contains everything the cat needs for healthy eating. At least the manufacturers, who are subject to federal and state pet food regulations, must give the exact composition on the label. Still, these days it's an issue, not only for that reason but for the quality of the products from which the food is pro-

duced. Only high-quality ingredients should be processed. The "critical user's eye" is also required. Some cats like one brand and can't stand another or even vomit it up. Therefore, choose very carefully among the different options.

A good quality cat food should provide all the elements your cat needs, except water. Because nutritional needs are different at the various stages of life, adjust the food to the age range of your cat. Because your cat needs a

HOW-TO:
Feeding

How the Cat Eats

The way in which a house cat takes in food and fluids comes from its wild existence. Respect your cat's eating habits, also taking into consideration that your pet must be pleased with what you place before it.

Eating

The cat usually crouches while eating, with the front and back legs bent, the rear end slightly raised, and the tail stretched out straight or tidily curled around the body.

If several cats are living together, each should have its own dish in order to get its full share. For example, one may just gobble the food, whereas the other may be a more thoughtful eater. Your pet may take the food out of the dish morsel by morsel, sometimes put it back down again next to the dish, sniff it extensively, and only then eat it. While doing so the cat may turn its head to the side, looking as if eating were something sneaky.

Drinking

The cat can shape its long, flexible tongue like a spoon. It scoops up the water and brings it to its mouth. The movement is so deft that you can scarcely follow it with the naked eye.

Grooming

When the cat has eaten, it first thoroughly licks around its mouth. If that isn't enough, it then uses its tongue to dampen its paw and "washes" its face clean.

How Much the Cat Eats

• A kitten between seven and 12 weeks should be fed five times a day and can polish off up to 8.75 ounces (250 g). If your pet is obviously thriving and not vomiting, it needs the food for which it's constantly begging. With increasing age, cut back on the number of feedings but not on the quantity.

• An adolescent cat between the age of three and seven months can tolerate up to 12.5 ounces (350 g) per day without adding fat. Divide the food into two to three meals per day but don't give anything between meals.

• As soon as the indoor cat is grown (body weight between 7.75 and 11 pounds, you should reduce the quantity of food and the number of meals. The cat doesn't need more than 4.5 ounces (130 g) per day divided into two feedings, or a quarter of a cup of dried food. If the cat is especially large or especially lively, you can increase the food quantity to 5.25 to 7 ounces (150 to 200 g) per day.

• A pregnant cat must not receive much more food, but the food should be nutrient-rich and divided into four to five portions during the day. A cat that's nursing kittens however, needs decidedly more food, approximately 15.75 ounces (450 g), likewise divided into several meals.

What the Cat Eats

The following tips and directions as well as the recipes for the preparation of simple cat menus come from personal experience. But each cat responds differently, so you must try out each one to see whether your cat will like it.

Practical Preparation Tips

• Meat from horses, sheep, rabbits, or game must be fresh and from unimpeachable sources, and must always be served to your cat cooked (see Fresh Food, page 44).

• The cat needs nutrient-rich but not necessarily "tasty" food in a

human sense. Therefore, go easy on the salt and other seasonings.

• To provide vitamin A, the cat needs 3.5 to 5.25 ounces (100 to 150 g) of liver per week. Keep portion-size amounts in the freezer and daily mix one portion into the food.

• Once a week, a teaspoon of olive oil or margarine in the food will ensure that the cat doesn't vomit up hair balls but excretes them instead.

• If you change the weight measurements in the following recipes into cup measurements, you will have less work.

Simple Recipes for Cat Menus

The quantities given provide the food requirements for one day.

Meat Dish

3.5 ounces (100 g) meat of horse, sheep, rabbit, or game, or pork or beef, cooked and minced into cat-sized bites
2 Tbs 6-grain baby cereal
1 tsp yeast-vitamin-flakes
2 Tbs pureed carrots (baby food)
1 Tbs liver
1 Tbs oil or margarine

Fish Dish

3.5 ounces (100 g) frozen fish steamed in water
1 Tbs cooked rice
1 tsp oil or margarine
2 Tbs cooked vegetables
1 tsp yeast flakes

Poultry Dish

3.5 ounces (100 g) cooked chicken cut into cat-size bites
1 Tbs cottage cheese
1 tsp oil or margarine
2 Tbs pureed carrots (baby food)
1 tsp yeast-vitamin-flakes
1 Tbs liver

Viscera Dish

3.5 ounces (100 g) of turkey or beef heart, cooked and cut into cat-sized bites
2 Tbs cooked vegetables
1 tsp oil or margarine
1 Tbs liver
1 tsp yeast-vitamin-flakes
1 Tbs cottage cheese

Eating Habits

• Regularly feed at the same time. Cats count on it.

• Don't let the food stand around for too long. Divide the day's ration into appropriately small portions. (For 4 ounces [120 g] and two meals, that's 2 ounces [60 g] at a time.)

• Don't give food directly from the refrigerator.

• Keep food varied and interesting. For dieting, don't make the cat fast but measure out smaller portions.

• Don't let yourself be manipulated into feeding outside the regular times (see HOW-TO: Training, page 30).

• Leftovers from your own meals must not be too highly spiced, too salty, or too sweet.

• Wash out the feeding bowl each time with hot water. Don't use any soaps or detergents.

• Dog food isn't good for cats over an extended period, because it contains much less protein.

well-balanced and comprehensive diet to provide all the elements it needs to remain healthy, you should provide a good quality cat food, and not rely wholly on meat, cans of tuna, table scraps, or snacks. Don't give your cat raw meat because of the risk of acquiring toxoplasma tissue cysts, which can lead to the disease toxoplasmosis. Raw meat can also contain parasites such as *Trichinella spiralis*, which causes the disease trichinosis.

Avoid feeding your cat only one type of food—for example, always feeding tuna-only entrees, or all-liver dinners. Such exclusive diets cause dietary diseases—cats need a variety of food sources in order to get complete nutrition.

After every meal, the cat licks its mouth thoroughly clean.

Different Forms of Food Available

Ready-made food is offered in various forms:
• Moist food in cans offers complete nutrition and consists of a mixture of muscle meat, viscera, or various ocean fish, with additional vegetable protein, grains, minerals, and vitamins.

My tip: Because the soft consistency of this food offers too little challenge to the cat's teeth and gums, tartar can build up and gum disease may develop. So, alternate with dry food and give the cat freshly prepared food every now and then.
• Dry food is a highly concentrated complete diet that contains approximately 10 percent water.

Cats must drink a great deal of water if they are fed with this, and therefore you must be sure a dish of water is always available. As a rule of thumb, for every 3.5 ounces (100 g) of dry food, provide 100 milliliters of water. Cats are not world champion drinkers, so often the amount of water they take in isn't enough to compensate for the fluid deficit. Neutered males, who have a tendency to bladder stones and life-threatening urinary blockage, suffer particularly from this and may incur damage.

My tip: For neutered males, only offer dry food as additional nibbling food, very sparingly, so that the cat has something to chew on for its teeth now and then. Or, you can choose a dry cat food that is low in magnesium and phosphorus, the suspected culprits of feline urological syndrome, and feed it regularly along with a good quality canned cat food.

Fresh Food

Fresh food offers a change from canned food in any case. The balancing

When two cats get along with each other, there's no rivalry at the feeding dish.

of the nutrients is important, for a one-sided diet of only meat can lead to deficiency disease. The following must be taken into consideration:

Meat: Raw meat is the most natural food for a cat. But because of the danger of disease transmission, veterinarians have come to advise against it. Pork can contain the organism causing the deadly Aujeszky's disease (pseudorabies); beef may be infected with the toxoplasma protozoan parasite that causes toxoplasmosis; poultry and eggs may contain salmonella.

Viscera: Only feed boiled heart (without fat), lungs, and kidneys; wash kidneys well. Raw liver has a laxative effect; cooked liver has just the opposite.

Fish: Only offer lightly steamed and boned fish once a week or the cat will smell of it. Raw fish contains an enzyme that can cause vitamin B-1 deficiency.

Fat: Mix easily digestible fats like corn, wheat germ, or sunflower oil or margarine into the food.

Fluids and Opportunities to Drink

Cats drink little water and in general get enough liquid from their food so that their requirements are met. You should always have a filled dish of fresh water available for your cat so that it doesn't drink the standing water out of the toilet, watering cans, or plant saucers. Some cats have their own peculiarities. My Nina, for instance, loves to stand directly under the water faucet.

Illness: Prevention and Care

E ven if your indoor cat isn't apt to be infected with disease by another cat, you should have the animal regularly immunized against the most dangerous infectious diseases. Even people can transmit disease.

People say that cats are by nature more robust, hardy, and resistant to disease than other animals. This most certainly applies to indoor cats, who of course lead a much more protected life than free-roaming cats. Many owners of indoor cats don't know what a sick cat is. You may be among them too if you take good care of your velvetpaws, feed and maintain your pet properly, and above all treat your pet lovingly and considerately. But there are also a few preventive measures you should take regardless. If kitty doesn't encounter anything untoward, your cat may live for 14 years or longer.

Immunization, the Best Prevention

Immunization shots are the most important and the most valuable preventative measures for your cat, even if it's only kept indoors and doesn't come into contact with other cats. For immunization, the animal must be healthy and free of parasites. Have your cat

Illness can express itself in many ways. Most noticeable to the pet owner are the cat's behavior changes.

checked for internal parasites with a fecal analysis performed by your veterinarian before the immunization. The veterinarian is the only one who can administer the shots. He or she enters it in an immunization record and notes at the same time when you should take your cat for booster shots.

Immunization injections are available against:
• Panleukopenia, also called feline infectious enteritis. This very infectious viral disease is not only transmitted from animal to animal but also by intermediate carriers, even by hands, shoes, and other objects.
• Feline respiratory diseases. There are only shots for the most virulent viruses. Proof is usually only required by boarding kennels.
• Feline leukemia. It is transmitted from cat to cat (bites, licking, copulation). It is diagnosed with a test performed by the veterinarian.
• Rabies. It is contagious to humans. Immunization is required for foreign travel, showing, and boarding. Some states require you to immunize your pets.
• Feline infectious peritonitis (FIP). This disease is often accompanied by increasing abdominal water retention. An effective and safe intranasal vaccine is now available for FIP.

Note: There are no immunizations against pseudorabies, for instance, and against feline AIDS. The feline immunodeficiency virus (FIV) of course belongs to the same group of viruses as the human AIDS virus, but it has been established that it does not threaten

Immunization Chart

	Age	Feline Panleukopenia	Respiratory Illnesses	Leukemia	Rabies	FIP
Basic Immunization	8 weeks	•	•	•		
	12 weeks	•	•	•		
	16 weeks				•	
	19 weeks					•
	after 1 year	•	•	•	•	•
	after 2 years		•	•	•	•
	after 3 years	•	•	•	•	•
	after 4 years		•	•	•	•

Important: Immunizations are not effective immediately. It takes about one to two weeks for the immunity to develop.

people. So you need have no fear and need not get rid of your cat if it is diagnosed with FIV. Let the veterinarian suggest what you can do for your cat.

Worming

A young kitten usually doesn't have worms if its mother is free of them. But only the veterinarian can tell for sure when you bring the kitten's stool sample at the time of immunization. If necessary, he or she will then prescribe or administer worming medication (preparations in injection or tablet form). With indoor cats, who can only be newly infected with difficulty, the worming treatment will not have to be repeated.

Diseases Communicable to Humans

There's a long list of diseases that can attack humans and cats. An indoor cat that is immunized and only eats cooked or prepared food rarely picks up pathogens that can also be dangerous for you.

Rabies: In principle, only cats that go outdoors must be immunized against rabies. But immunization will also be necessary if you travel, and some areas require that you vaccinate your cat. Because the requirements vary from state to state, you should find out ahead of time (veterinarian, or, if out of the country, the embassy or consulate).

Toxoplasmosis: This is dangerous for pregnant women, whose unborn fetus may incur serious damage to brain and eyes from the disease. Women should therefore tell their doctor about the cat at the very beginning of the pregnancy and have their blood checked for toxoplasmosis twice at intervals of six weeks.

My tip: For the duration of the pregnancy, avoid close body contact with your cat and let someone else attend to the litter box. But you don't by any means have to get rid of your cat.

Ringworm: Caused by a skin fungus, ringworm manifests itself with falling hair and itching. You must take your pet to

The cat may nibble on cypress grass.

Diarrhea can be a symptom of illness.

Further signs of good health are a thick, shining coat; clear eyes; clean ears (inside as well); undamaged teeth without any tartar deposits; pink gums without any bad odor or line of red near the teeth; formed, soft, dark stool; and yellow, unclouded urine.

A sick cat, on the other hand, sits around listlessly, doesn't eat, and may scratch itself constantly. Further signs that indicate ill health or disease are, among others, constant thirst, diarrhea, persistent vomiting, fever, coughing, and severe weight loss. If you notice any of these symptoms, you should not put off going to the veterinarian.

Going to the Veterinarian

Finding a veterinarian is a matter of confidence. After all, you must bring your cat in for immunization shots and checkups at least once a year. You should find a specialist who understands about cats. If you get a referral from another cat owner, your breeder, or from a cat breeding association, your choice will be a little easier.

Transport: Bring your cat to the veterinarian in the cat carrier. Keep the cat in the carrier while in the waiting room.

Consultation: Give the veterinarian a brief report of the symptoms and answer his or her questions precisely. For instance:

• How's your cat eating?
• Does your pet drink more than usual?
• Has the cat vomited more often than usual? Does it have diarrhea or constipation (if possible bring along a stool sample)?
• Does your pet sit around passively; does it neglect its grooming; is it unclean?
• Have you taken your cat's temperature and if so, how high is it?
• Does the cat scratch a lot, for instance at its ears, or does it keep shaking its head?

the veterinarian for treatment. To prevent reinfection, thoroughly disinfect the cat's bed, comb, brush, and toys, and everything the cat has touched. Sometimes these things have to be thrown away. Observe careful hygiene and wash your hands after each contact with your cat, for you can be infected yourself.

When the Cat Gets Sick

A healthy cat is lively, curious, playful, and regularly and thoroughly grooms itself from top to bottom.

- Has the cat had an accident?
- Does your pet cough much?
- Has the cat lost a lot of weight?

If the veterinarian prescribes medications, administer the dosages exactly and continue to give the medication even if the illness disappears after only half the time period has elapsed. Follow all other doctor's orders exactly.

What the Cat Owner Can Do

Kitty is sick. Now your cat needs a cozy bed, proper care, and your encouragement so that your pet will soon be healthy again. A cat isn't a patient patient, and it won't be evident to your pet that everything being done is in its best interest. Therefore, you must make use of all kinds of tricks. Here are the most important care measures:

Sickbed: A shallow carton or cat bed with a slightly raised edge makes a good sickbed so that the cat can't fall out; furnish it with a soft cushion and cover this with a washable cloth that can be changed.

Location: Place the sickbed in a warm, draft-free place where you can take care of the patient comfortably. If there are other cats there, keep the sick cat isolated in the case of contagious diseases.

Feeding: Feed your cat fresh, warmed delicacies or good-tasting concentrated food (available from the veterinarian). If the cat can't chew, puree the food. Sometimes it may have to be fed. Slowly trickle slightly salted meat or chicken broth with a syringe (without a needle) or eye dropper sideways in behind the canine teeth. Don't spray in a surge or the cat may choke.

Drinking: Fresh drinking water must always be within reach. If the sick cat doesn't drink enough, you'll have to administer water with the syringe.

A cat beauty with clear eyes and a spotless coat.

Tablets, pills, capsules: A cat will let itself be fooled just once by a tablet being hidden in a tasty morsel of food (break up large tablets into smaller particles). But once your pet's seen through it, you can try the following procedure: Hold the tablet ready in one hand between your thumb and index finger while with the other hand you grasp the animal's head with light pressure behind the teeth. The cat will then involuntarily open its mouth. Now insert the tablet as far back on the tongue as possible and massage your

Y ou should master some important maneuvers for dealing with the feline patient. Among them are the administration of medicine as well as taking its temperature.

pet's throat gently downward until you can feel the tablet being swallowed.

Drops: Trickle drops on the cat's paw, so that your pet may possibly lick the drops up all by itself, provided they taste good. Bitter medications can be instilled with a syringe (see Feeding, above).

Taking temperatures: It's easiest to manage taking your cat's temperature with two people. While one holds the cat by the shoulder and forepaws and speaks calmingly to the animal, the other lifts its tail a little and inserts the thermometer, which has been lubricated with petroleum jelly (a digital thermometer is best), as horizontally as possible about three quarters of an inch into the anus, leaving it there for two minutes. The temperature of a healthy cat is between 100 and 102.6° F (37.8–39.2° C).

Counting the pulse: The pulse is best felt on the inside of the thigh, with one hand stroking and the other hand feeling the pulse beat. Normally it should be between 110 and 140 beats per minute.

Eye salves: Hold the cat's head firmly at the back and at the same time carefully draw back the upper eyelid with your index finger. Lay a line of salve about a quarter of an inch under the lid.

Never touch the eyeball directly with the tip of the tube.

Eye- and eardrops: To instill drops in the eyes, firmly hold the cat's head from behind, at the same time carefully withdrawing the bottom eyelid with your index finger. Let two to three drops trickle from the dropper bottle to behind the lid. Be careful not to touch the eyeball directly.

When instilling drops in the ear, carefully hold up the pinna of the ear and let four to five drops trickle into the auditory canal. Then gently massage the ear at the base so that the fluid will distribute itself throughout the canal.

Injections: A cat suffering from diabetes must receive a daily injection. Let the veterinarian teach you the correct procedure. When you are skilled, the cat will hardly feel it. A friend told me that her cat even regularly presents the "shot spot" at the right time.

Treatment of Simple Health Problems

When your cat is sick, you should get quick, expert help from the veterinarian. But you can also do a few things. Many of the natural remedies mentioned below can be obtained from a pharmacy or health food store.

Mild diarrhea (runny stools; when accompanied by vomiting, get to the veterinarian at once). If you believe the cause of the diarrhea is dietary, change your cat's menu. (Such foods as whole milk, raw liver, or spoiled meat may cause diarrhea and should not be part of your cat's diet.) For treatment of mild cases, you might try boiled rice water mixed with cottage cheese or cat food. Some veterinarians recommend that you give your cat nothing to eat for 24 hours, then feed bland food for a week. If no improvement in 24 hours, go to the veterinarian. Kittens with diarrhea should always be seen by a veterinarian immediately because they become dehydrated so quickly.

Mild constipation (difficulty moving bowels): Long-haired cats often suffer from mild constipation. One teaspoon of olive oil in its food once or twice may be enough to take care of this, or use a cat laxative available from your vet. Improvement should occur after two days. If there is also vomiting present, go to the veterinarian.

Coughing: Coughing is usually a sign of hairballs. There are commercial hairball remedies available in pet stores and the pet food section of supermarkets, and they are usually effective when directions are carefully followed. If no improvement occurs, go to the veterinarian.

Eye inflammation: When lids are swollen, bathe the corner of the eye carefully three to four times daily with euphrasia (ten drops in a glass of lukewarm water). If no improvement within two days, go to the veterinarian.

Bruises (after a fall): An ice pack will probably prevent swelling, or alternate poultices of arnica or calendula tincture (thin carefully).

Superficial wounds: Apply tincture of calendula salve or aloe vera.

Treatment of shock after accidents: In this important life-saving first aid measure, lay the cat on its right side (of course only if it has no external wounds there) on a blanket or towel, carefully supporting the neck and rump from the back as you lift. Wrap the blanket around the animal and place your pet comfortably in a basket or on your lap. Keep the head somewhat lower than the rest of the body so that the brain remains filled with blood. In this way, transport the animal to the veterinarian, who has been informed of the accident.

The Old Cat

You've lived with your cat for many years and mainly have been dealing with a sturdy, vital animal. But now that's your pet is old, its health needn't necessarily be bad. The old cat probably won't move so agilely. For example, your pet might not leap up to its usual high places, but may prefer a soft pillow that it can reach comfortably. The old cat will probably eat less and become thinner, and it won't groom as often and may have a rough coat. At this period of its life, your pet's environment should be changed as little as possible. The excitement of a young kitten is stressful for your old cat; a move can be terrifying.

Care: Be loving to your animal, that's the main thing. And have the veterinarian look at it every three or four months. An aging cat can suffer from constipation or have problems with its teeth, and its sight and hearing gradually diminish. Other diseases, such as kidney disfunction and hyperthyroidism,

In many illnesses, warmth is good for the cat. Put a soft cushion in the cat bed and a washable towel over it.

are common in older cats. Any physical or behavior changes should be discussed with your veterinarian.

Euthanasia: However, when the cat becomes ill and has great pain, you should discuss with the veterinarian whether putting it to sleep isn't the best solution. Only your vet is able to administer a euthanizing injection. The cat will only feel the slight prick of the needle and if you are there holding your pet in your arms, it will pass away very peacefully.

Learning to Understand Cats

Cats' Capabilities

People never grow tired of marveling at the incomparable litheness of the cat body: the relaxation and ease in the sleeping position, the fervent stretching and lolling after awakening, the coiled-spring stalking run, the pliant agility with which the cat slips itself through cracks and holes, or the acrobatic contortions performed in grooming. All the other things the cat is able to do are no less amazing.

Leaping: From a standing position, the cat can jump five times its own height. In doing so, your pet estimates the distance so exactly that it lands right where it wanted to, such as right in the middle of a fully laden mantelpiece without breaking anything. Jumping down, your pet leans so far forward that it almost seems as though the cat is walking down the wall. By this maneuver, it shortens the distance to the floor.

Falling: The cat's ability to fall and land on its feet is legendary. If it falls backward, it can resume its normal position with lightning speed, that is, using its tail as rudder and brake, it turns in free fall, first the front part of its body, then the rear, curving its back in order to lessen the impact, and lands on all four feet.

Running: The cat moves as "quietly as a cat," that is, it only touches the floor with its toes, with the effect being increased by the ball of the foot's padding. The velvety soft paws are furnished with needle-sharp claws, which on the front paws are retractable. They

Aren't you going to let me into the basket? The kittens practice instinctive behavior patterns in play.

are not ground down in walking and always remain sharp.

Balancing: The certainty with which a cat balances its way across a curtain rod is marvelous. It uses its tail to balance itself, rather the way a tightrope walker uses his staff.

Sensory Abilities

The most fascinating thing about cats are their eyes, large amber yellow, copper-colored, violet blue, or emerald green pools. But they are not only wonderfully beautiful, they perform astonishingly.

Seeing: The size of the eye permits a kind of panoramic viewing, that is, while looking straight ahead, the cat see everything moving except just behind its ears. As a hunter, the cat's perception is based on movement. In the area with its best depth of focus (between 6.5 and 20 feet), the cat can distinguish the hurrying ant, whereas a mouse playing dead may entirely escape your pet. Furthermore, the cat can see when you can no longer see your hands in front of your face. In darkness, the cat's pupils become very large and collect a maximum of light. The brighter it is, the more they narrow until they are no more than a slit. A reflective layer in the rear of the eye amplifies the effect of the entering light. That's why cats' eyes glow like lamps when they are caught in a beam of light in the darkness.

Hearing: The cat hears in frequency ranges up to 65 kHz (the human only hears to 20 kHz) and perceives such

These two understand each other. The pedagogical value of an animal for the development of the child is uncontested. The child learns to take responsibility for another living being and her compassion and sense of duty are developed.

In dealing with a cat, children learn to respect the personality of the animal.

HOW-TO:
Understanding Cat Language

Cat language is a combination of sounds and body language. Kitty expresses its mood with its body. In addition, your pet vocalizes to express its mood. The following descriptions may sharpen your understanding of feline language so that you can comprehend what your "human-cat" is trying to tell you.

Feeling Good

The cat sits or lies there with a friendly, relaxed expression. Its ears are aimed forward and slightly spread; its whiskers aim sideways and are a little spread out. Its eyes look calm and sparkle, depending on the brightness. In greeting, kitty will come to you with tail upright and head raised. If your pet wants to cuddle with you, it closes its eyes and,

1] A toy has attracted this cat's attention. Playfully it swings at the interesting object.

purring, rubs its head and flanks against your legs. Or your cat butts its head against your hand.

Alertness
Drawing 1

It's not the wide-eyed gaze that shows the cat is excited. It's that your pet's ears are erect and pointing forward. Its whiskers are also aimed forward and spread wide. At the moment, the cat appears very quiet, only its tail waves gently back and forth. It lifts a paw to swing playfully at the thing that has caught its attention.

Defense
Drawing 2

The signs of defense are subtle at the beginning, and if they aren't properly understood, you may experience some painful misunderstandings. For instance, if kitty doesn't want to be disturbed in its sleeping spot, the cat at first signals reserve, with ears laid sideways, pupils enlarged, and whiskers pulled back. If you overlook these signs, those velvet paws become weapons of defense, with claws extended to deliver painful scratches. At the same time, the cat hisses and spits, or growls deep in its throat, which increases to a shrill scream, depending on the degree of rage or fear.

Aggression
Drawing 3

Aggressive behavior mainly occurs between one cat and another. With indoor cats that have grown up together and know each other, it is usually a

2] Ears flattened, pupils enlarged, whiskers laid back—kitty is angry and is also lashing out with her paws.

matter of challenging one another's territory, or play fighting. On stiffened legs, one plants itself before the other, turns back its erect ears, its whiskers spread wide and its pupils narrowed. Its tail is bent down hooklike just behind the root and its fur is fluffed out so that it looks like a bottle brush. The cat crouches at right angles and then throws itself on the other cat. That cat rolls lightning fast onto its back and parries with teeth and claws. But if the cat just doesn't want to fight, it drops its head and thus signals submission. In disinterest, it turns its head to the side.

Anxious Shyness
Drawing 4

If a cat withdraws into a hiding place in anxious shyness, it's trying to make itself inconspicuous for a while. Its ears are laid to the side and its whiskers are pulled back against its cheeks. Eyes and pupils are small, its chin is pressed in. The cat's face looks "drawn in" as does its whole body. You'll see these signs particularly in cats from the animal shelter. If it becomes fearful, it quickly goes into a defensive posture. You should know this if you try to touch an anxious cat. Its fur bristles, its ears lay back flat on its head, its pupils become gigantic, its tail lashes back and forth, and it may even let out a loud screech. Just talk reassuringly, don't touch the cat unless you want a few bloody scratches.

Sound Language

Cat language isn't complete without sounds that kitty sometimes uses outspokenly in relationship to its people. The language of sounds enhances and underlines body language and mimicry, expresses well-being, happiness, and affection, but also bad temper, defense, enmity, and aggression.

Meow: The cat says meow in all tones and gradations, to express complaints, demands, questions, and excitement. If kit-

tens feel abandoned, their meows sound very high, like, "miii, miii."

Purring: Expressing well-being and a feeling of security, kittens purr when they drink. Mother cats purr when they nurse and lick their young. Young felines invite adult cats and people to play with them. Cats that are friends purr when they meet, and subordinate cats when they approach dominant ones to acknowledge their inferiority. But cats also purr in sickness and severe pain, and, indeed, even shortly before death.

Cooing: It's a kind of conversational language with many variations that cats have available for every possible life situation. In cooing, the cat asks its people for attention, and with gentle cooing the mother cat summons her kittens.

Spitting: Uttered with the nose wrinkled, spitting means enmity.

Growling: This noise is a warning to an opponent. A cat growls when it doesn't want to be disturbed while eating.

Chattering: The cat chatters when it looks through the window and discerns a bird or fly that it can't reach. Then it utters a staccato chattering sound and clacks its teeth regularly.

Ranking

Ranking develops when several cats live together. Usually there are one or two top cats who own the best sleeping places and are first at the feeding dishes. They claim the dish of their choice, whereas the others share the remaining dishes. Ranking is communicated through body language. For example, top cats frequently hit the other members of their social group in the

4] Ears turned to the side, whiskers laid back, eyes narrowed, this cat is afraid, and so it withdraws anxiously into a hiding place.

face in a gesture of dominance. It also appears that cats forget their rank, and at times the subordinate cat may temporarily take the place of the dominant one. The social order can also change. For example, a spayed or neutered cat will lose its social standing. A cat can also lose its rank if it is removed from the environment for a time, for example, an extended hospital stay or by being boarded.

3] The facial expression of this cat signifies belligerence. Angry spitting reinforces its mood.

Should I grab him? the cat appears to be asking herself.

fine sounds as the squeaking, pattering, and gnawing of mice. Even when asleep, the cat reacts immediately to strange sounds.

Sense of touch: If you were to cut off a cat's whiskers, it could no longer find its way through a hole. It measures the width of the opening with these sensitive "antennae" and thus knows whether it will become stuck. The whiskers are its guiding system, so that it doesn't bump into any chair legs in the dark.

Smelling: The Jacobson's organ permits the cat a kind of smell-tasting. By smelling, it develops a "picture" of every new person, every strange cat, and of course of its environment. By rubbing with its head, chin, tail, and feet, the cat leaves behind scent information, for example, on its scratching post and furniture or throughout its circuits around the house, fortunately

"readable" only by other cats.

Taste: The sense of taste isn't as developed in the cat. Probably your cat fixates on a certain food less because of taste than from habit and because the odor appeals to it. The cat can differentiate the taste of salt, but it has no special sense for sweet. However, it nibbles on the whipped cream tart on the table because it can't help snitching. It has many little bumps on its tongue called taste papillae, which feel like sandpaper when the cat licks you in a friendly manner on the face.

Interpreting Instinctive Behavior Patterns

It is a brightly lit day and your cat sits there staring at you with wide-open eyes. Uneasily you wonder what your cat is thinking because cats' pupils should really only be large at night (see

Better not! He does have a terrifically strong beak, after all.

About the photos: Getting an "old inhabitant" apartment cat and a new arrival used to each other can be promblematical. It works best with a young kitten. With its impetuous curiosity and its marked drive to play, the new kitten will soon have won the "oldster" over.

Sensory Abilities, page 52). If, on the other hand, you know that the cat usually opens its eyes wide when it's worried, you needn't worry about it and perhaps only have to seek out the reason for its concern. Learn to read the innate behavior patterns of your cat correctly, and you will have still more pleasure in your life together and more often view the world as your cat might view it.

Purring

The cat appears to express well-being by purring. But that isn't entirely right. It means more "I'm in a friendly mood" than "I'm content." In its primoridal function, purring reports to the nursing mother that the kittens are well. Once grown up, the cat still purrs but changes the meaning according to the situation and the social circumstances. Mother cats purr during nursing and grooming their young; kittens purr when they invite adult cats or people to play. Friendly cats purr at every meeting, dominant animals when they peacefully approach subordinate ones. Sick and very weak cats purr for comfort.

Kneading

The cat has sprawled on your lap and after a short time it begins slowly and with regular alternation to press down with both front paws. When you also feel its sharp claws and notice that the cat is drooling, finally you push your pet aside. This kneading is a relic of kittenhood. To get the flow of milk started, the kittens massage the belly of the mother with their tiny paws. Adult cats, who see their owners as their adoptive parents so to speak, therefore repeat the childish behavior pattern and feel themselves correspondingly ill-used if they are rejected.

The position of the ears and whiskers signals alertness.

This posture betrays growing unrest.

Licking

The cat cleans and licks its coat many times a day to rid itself of dust and dead fur. After every meal, it licks its mouth clean and then washes its face with a dampened paw. But also sometimes the cat briefly licks up over its nose or its coat where there is nothing to groom—a quick swipe of the tongue, comparable to your scratching your head. You may do it when you're perplexed and don't know exactly how to decide something. Similarly, the cat licks it when it doesn't know what to do, whether to run or stay. The conflict is not easy to solve, the tension of it so great that the cat carries out some kind of substitute behavior. This is also called displacement grooming.

Rubbing

The cat rubs closely around your legs in greeting. How nice, you think. However, it isn't just friendly body contact but has another meaning. When the cat rubs forehead, cheeks, flanks, and tail on a human's legs, it's exchanging body odors with you. Your pet has perfumed you with the special scent glands that are located on its temples, corners of the mouth, and root of the tail. You can't smell it, however, because these scents are too subtle for your nose. But to cats, these scents are very important, for through them they feel themselves bonded closer to "their" people. Because afterward they are usually in the habit of grooming very intensively, they also continue to take up your scent with their tongues.

Scratching

When the cat sharpens its claws on your favorite chair it isn't doing that to annoy you. One of the reasons your pet scratches is scent-marking (see Scratching and Climbing Equipment, page 18). The cat has scent glands on the underside of the front paws that in scratching are rubbed hard on the furniture. And if it scratches its "name" on your chair, your pet wants to add its scent to yours and at the same time express its affection. Thus if your pet continues to ignore the scratching equipment that's pointed out, it sometimes helps to hang a cast-off T-shirt over the post.

Behavior Problems

If your cat suddenly starts doing things it's never done before—urinating on the carpet, nibbling on plants, or scratching furniture or rugs—you are understandably disturbed and angry. Problems of this sort can appear out of the blue, even with cats that previously have been very well behaved, and can severely disturb the harmony of your life together. Cats that have been adopted from an animal shelter and were previously abused or frightened can also change frighteningly sometimes. Before you undertake any drastic measures, you should be aware that such powerful reactions almost always have a cause that is often easy to remove.

The Unclean Cat

If your cat suddenly starts leaving messes on the carpet, there can be several reasons.

Sickness or age: The cat's normal behavior pattern is disturbed due to sickness or age and it urgently needs the veterinarian.

Litter box: If the litter box is dirty and the cat can't find any clean place to go anymore, or the litter box is in the wrong place such as next to the feeding dishes, a mess can occur. Cats hate to defecate where they eat. Or the litter pan is placed in a location where there are always people going by. That also goes against the cats' grain, for they prefer to be unobserved.

Disturbance of the usual routine: An intrusion in the household is one of the most common reasons for uncleanliness. Perhaps there were workers in the house who've been noisy and made a change in the daily environment. Perhaps you've bought new furniture. To the cat, this appears at first to be endangering its territory. Perhaps a second kitten has arrived and the old inhabitant must show its dominance with visible deposits of scat. You must restrengthen the self-confidence of your cat by showering it with affection. At the same time, clean the "piddle spot" so that your pet can't recognize it again, otherwise the cat will continue to use it. After cleaning the spot with soap and water or vinegar water, cover it—with a piece of plastic wrap, for instance—and spray it with mint or lemon oil, a scent that almost every cat hates. Scolding, screaming, or clapping doesn't help at all to prevent it and only upsets your cat even more.

My tip: Don't use any cleaning materials that contain ammonia. These smell like urine, which will immediately impel the cat to renew its own scent at the place that has just been cleaned.

Behavior disturbances: It's very difficult to find out the reason for behavior upsets. Sometimes it helps to give the cat another spot for a few weeks, for then often the uncleanliness will stop abruptly. But there isn't a completely reliable recipe.

Avoidance of Scratching Equipment

Wrong place: If the cat doesn't pass the scratching post on its circuit through the home, it has chosen another spot. Breaking the habit may not be easy now. Try the following:
• Cover the scratched place on the furniture, rug, or wallpaper with a smooth sheet of plastic. The cat won't like that. Move the scratching equipment to the vicinity.
• Move the maltreated furniture and put the scratching equipment in its place.
• Move the favorite sleeping spot to the vicinity of the scratching equipment.
• Nail a piece of sisal rug over the scratching spot, if that's possible.
• Make a sacrifice, as it were, of the now scratched piece of furniture and every day move it a few more inches into a corner.

Starting too late: If you only install the scratching equipment after the cat has developed its habit, accept the blame and try gently to change your pet's habit.

Nibbling on Plants

Cats, especially long-haired cats, need something green, probably to vomit up the fur swallowed during grooming. Place a pot of grass just for the cat—they love to eat cypress grass (*Cyperus alternifolius*), or oat grass, for example—and get your pet accustomed to this grass early. To keep your cat from getting confused about which plants it may nibble on and which it may not, you should place the grass far away from your favorite houseplants. Praise the cat when it eats its grass; call "No!" when your pet attacks your plants.

But the cat will also begin to chew on plants out of boredom, for instance when it's alone all day. You'll need to provide more variety for the cat (see HOW-TO: Playing, page 38 and Arranging Your Home for a Cat, page 16), and to protect your plants, if only because some of them may be poisonous (see the list). Try protecting your plants with:
• Mothballs, sewn into little bags, hanging on the plants;

The position of the ears creates an almost horizontal line. The cat is threatening to attack.

The ears bent sideways and a wicked snarl tell the opponent: ready for attack.

Poisonous Plants: Amaryllis, bird-of-paradise, belladonna, black locust, caladium, castor bean, chinaberry, daffodil, daphne, datura, elephants ear, euonymus, foxglove, fruit pits, golden chain, hemlock, henbane, holly, honeysuckle, hydrangea, Indian tobacco, iris, jack-in-the-pulpit, Jerusalem cherry, jimsonweed, larkspur, lily of the valley, marijuana, mescal bean, mistletoe, monkshood, moonseed, morning glory, mushrooms, nightshade, nutmeg, oleander, periwinkle, peyote, philodendron, potato, rhubarb, skunk cabbage, tobacco, tulip, wisteria, yew

• Painting the leaves with a taste the cat hates. It of course mustn't be harmful to the plants and the cat.

The Aggressive Cat

Perhaps you've taken in a stray cat or a cat from an animal shelter that has had bad experiences in its life. You must show it through your love and affection that life is going to be better from now on.

If a cat that until now has been a loving, cuddly cat suddenly develops the habit of attacking visitors and scratching and biting them, you must find out the cause.

Jealousy: Formerly a single person, you now have a partner, and that doesn't suit the cat at all. It's best if you now let the new person exclusively feed and stroke the cat. With time, the cat will accept the newcomer.

Fear: Cats also become aggressive out of fear. You can see it in their entire body language—ears flattened and laid back, large pupils. When they are at their wits' end, they spit and scratch and bite. Remove the cause of the fear and they again become gentle cuddly cats.

Sucking

When the just-acquired little kitten sucks on your finger or neck, you find that sweet. However, when the adult cat still retains this habit, it's less pleasant. If your pet sucks on fabric and yarn and your skin and hair, you should do something about the habit early on.

Put the cat aside as soon as it begins to suck. If your pet won't stop, say "No" and possibly underline the command with a light tap with a rolled-up newspaper. Be consistent about refusing to let the cat suck, or your attemps will be useless.

Many cats drink by catching the drops of water from an opened faucet.

Useful Addresses and Literature

Cat Associations

American Association of Cat
  Enthusiasts (AACE)
  P.O. Box 213
  Pine Brook, NJ 07058
  (201) 335-6717

American Cat Association (ACA)
  Dept. CF
  8101 Katherine Avenue
  Panorama City, CA 91402
  (818) 781-5656

American Cat Fanciers
  Association (ACFA)
  Dept. CF
  P.O. Box 203
  Pt. Lookout, MO 65726
  (417) 334-5430

Canadian Cat Association (CCA)
  Dept. CF
  83 Kennedy Road, Unit 1806
  Brampton, Ontario
  Canada L6W 3P3

**Other Organizations and Animal
Protection Agencies**

American Humane Association
  P.O. Box 1266
  Denver, CO 80201
  (303) 695-0811

American Society for the
  Prevention of Cruelty to
  Animals (ASPCA)
  424 East 92nd Street
  New York, NY 10128
  (212) 876-7700

Friends of Animals
  P.O. Box 1244
  Norwalk, CT 06856
  (800) 631-2212
  (for low cost spay/neuter
  program information)

The Humane Society of the
  United States (HSUS)
  2100 L St. N.W.
  Washington, DC 20037
  (202) 452-1100

Pets Are Wonderful Support
  (PAWS)
  P.O. Box 460489
  San Francisco, CA 94146
  (415) 241-1460
  (provides pet-related services
  for people with AIDS)

Cat Magazines

Cats
  P.O. Box 420240
  Palm Coast, FL 32142-0240
  (904) 445-2818

Cat Fancy
  P.O. Box 52864
  Boulder, CO 52864

Cat Fancier's Almanac
  1805 Atlantic Avenue
  P.O. Box 1005
  Manasquan, NJ 08736-0805
  (908) 528-9797

Catnip (newsletter)
  Tufts University School of
  Veterinary Medicine

P.O. Box 420014
Palm Coast, FL 32142-0014
(800) 829-0926

Books for Additional Reading

Behrend, K. and Wegler, Monika.
  *The Complete Book of Cat
  Care.* Barron's Educational
  Series, Inc., Hauppauge, New
  York: 1991.

Daly, Carol Himsel, D.V.M.
  Caring for Your Sick Cat.
  Barron's Educational Series,
  Inc., Hauppauge, New York:
  1994.

Frye, Fredric. *First Aid for Your
  Cat.* Barron's Educational
  Series, Inc., Hauppauge, New
  York: 1987.

Maggitti, Phil. *Guide to a
  Well-Behaved Cat.* Barron's
  Educational Series, Inc.,
  Hauppauge, New York: 1993.

Siegal, Mordecai and Cornell
  University. *The Cornell Book
  of Cats.* Villard Books, New
  York: 1989.

Viner, Bradley, D.V.M. *The Cat
  Care Manual.* Barron's
  Educational Series, Inc.,
  Hauppauge, New York: 1993.

Wright, M. and S., Walters, eds.
  The Book of the Cat. Summit
  Books, New York: 1980.

Index

The Author

Katrin Behrend, journalist, animal book editor, and author of successful German pet care books has recently moved to Italy to live and work. She has had cats, both house cats and purebred ones, for many years.

Thanks

The Author and Publisher thank Dr. Uwe Streitferdt for checking over the chapters "A Healthy Diet for Indoor Cats" and "Illness: Prevention and Care."

Cover Photos

Front cover: A real cat beauty.
Back cover: This cat is clearly enjoying the chance to cuddle up to the little girl.

Important Note

When dealing with cats, injuries from scratches and bites can occur. Have such injuries treated by a doctor immediately.

Don't neglect getting all necessary immunizations and wormings for your cat (see pages 46–47), because otherwise the health risks for people and animals are considerable. Some diseases and parasites are communicable to humans (see page 47). If your cat exhibits any signs of illness (see page 48), you should immediately seek the advice of a veterinarian. In any doubtful instances, you should yourself go to the doctor and indicate that you keep a cat. There are people who are allergic to cat hair. When in doubt, ask your doctor before you get a cat. There is the possibility that cats can injure other people's property or even cause accidents. An insurance policy to cover such risks is in your own interest. In any case you should carry liability insurance.

© Copyright 1994 by Grafe und Unzer GmbH, Munich. The title of the German book is *Die Wohnungskatze*. Translated from the German by Elizabeth D. Crawford. First English language edition published in 1995 by Barron's Educational Series, Inc.
English translation © Copyright 1995 by Barron's Educational Series, Inc.

Address all inquires to: Barron's Educational Series, Inc., 250 Wireless Boulevard, Hauppauge, New York 11788

Library of Congress Catalog Card No. 95-12976

International Standard Book Number 0-8120-9449-2

Library of Congress Cataloging-in-Publication Data
Behrend, Katrin.
      [Wohnungskatze. English]
   Indoor cats : understanding and taking care of your cat : expert advice for optimal care / Katrin Behrend ; color photographs, Ulrike Schanz ; drawings, Renate Holzner ; translation from the German, Elizabeth D. Crawford ; consulting editor, J. Anne Helgren.
         p.   cm.
   Includes bibliographical references (p.   ) and index.
      ISBN 0-8120-9449-2
   1. Cats. 2. Cats—Behavior. I. Helgren, J. Anne.
II. Title.
SF447.B4613   1995
636.8—dc20
                                                   95-12976
                                                       CIP

PRINTED IN HONG KONG

5678   9955   987654321